The Design
of the
Management
Information System

by DON Q MATTHEWS

AUERBACH ®
Publishers
Princeton   New York
Philadelphia   London

Library of Congress Catalog Card Number: 77-124629
Standard Book Number: 87769-049-9

First printing

Printed in the United States of America.

Contents

v

List of Figures

Preface

The management information system can potentially provide a significant new dimension in management practice. However, this potential can never be fully exploited until both the operating manager and the system analyst understand the nature of these systems and participate in establishing system objectives and basic system architecture. During the course of teaching computer science at the University of Tulsa, I have found an increasing need for a better understanding of management information systems, not only for business students but also for practicing managers and experienced computer analysts. This book is directed toward that need—an understanding of the design concepts and the problems associated with the amalgamation of management practice and computer science.

In actual practice it has been difficult to realize the full potential of the management information system. The design philosophies are quite different from either manual systems or conventional computer applications. The problems associated with managing the system development and the system implementation are also unique. There is, however, an increasing collection of design principles and administrative practices which apply to all types of organizations and to a broad range of management systems. This book does not attempt to describe how a computer works or to define management. Rather, it attempts to describe how to devise computerized management systems which will achieve the objectives of the organization. This should provide a middle ground for the business managers as they become more concerned with computer systems and for system analysts as they become increasingly involved in complex integrated management problems.

The book is organized so it may be used for self-study or classroom instruction. The system life cycle is introduced early in the book, as an understanding of this provides an insight into the larger system which is essential to the understanding of many design problems. The later chapters are largely self-contained so that they may be selected to fit a specific course structure or may be utilized for reference. Chapters 10, 11, and 12 survey some specific design methodologies and may be omitted by the reader who is familiar with these areas.

Grateful acknowledgment is due many associates and students who helped formulate the concepts, principles, and practices discussed, particularly the original MCS team at American Airlines. With so many people simultaneously working in this relatively new field, it is difficult to acknowledge the assistance of each. I am, however, especially grateful for the enthusiasm and confidence of Professor Anne Morrow, without which this work would never have been attempted, and to my wife, Charlotte, and my daughters, Pam and Lisa, for their continued patience and support.

The Design
of the
Management
Information System

1

Management and the Computer—An Overview

MODERN MANAGEMENT philosophies have become irreversibly intertwined with the computer. Organizational concepts, strategy, and decision making increasingly depend on a flow of information which can be generated only by the modern digital computer. There seems no end to the need for information about complex technology in a sophisticated society.

However, the computer is only a tool for advances in social and industrial organizations. The computer, despite its mystique, can do only what it has been instructed to do. The influence on society is the tasks for which we employ the computer—the systems which are devised by man to control his actions and their relationship with his fellow man. The computer has been the technological key to the exploitation of mathematical and scientific methodology in organizational operations. These techniques have been used to build increasingly sophisticated management systems which accurately and quickly evaluate alternatives, make decisions, and communicate information. The computer supplies the automation and speed characteristic of the systems, but be-

1

yond that it is rather incidental to the system design. It is the system itself which provides the means to achieve organizational objectives. Therefore, it must, of course, be tailored to the objectives and problems of the specific organization.

The need for information is universal. The computer terminal in the executive's office is no longer a prestige symbol but an essential work tool. The rapid availability of comprehensive and accurate information is changing many theories of organizational structure and operating practices. The impact of the computer on management in all segments of our society cannot be overemphasized.

MANAGEMENT SYSTEMS

The word "system" is common in contemporary vocabulary and is used in many fields to mean several things. We frequently hear such terms as "automation systems," "nervous systems," "social systems," "telephone systems," "weapons systems." In all these terms the word "system" does have some common connotations. One characteristic is the concept of a collection and orderly arrangement of elements or parts. The system is composed of a series of components which are interconnected in such a manner that there is cooperation between the activities of the various components and this cooperation occurs according to some predetermined set of rules.

Business organizations have developed over a long period of time a variety of systems to provide for their survival in an increasingly complex society. There are accounting systems, production systems, inventory systems, quality systems, and many others. Each of these systems plays an important part in the planning, direction, and control of the organization—the management of the organization. These systems, however, are not at all independent; they must be coordinated and interrelated in many elaborate and subtle ways to contribute to the common objectives of the organization. In fact, the modern business organization can be said to be defined literally as a system of systems. The management system must therefore be viewed as the total of these individual systems, including their interacting mechanisms.

Either independently or collectively, these functional systems generally display all the characteristics classically associated with a system. They all, however, also display certain characteristics which seem to place them in a special class of systems. Two predominant special characteristics are the interaction of man and machine and the environment of uncertainty and judgment within which they operate. The man and machine interface is present in all practical organizations, whether industrial, financial, institutional, and so on (even the "automated" refinery requires a human being to monitor the controls). No matter how complex the machine, the man plays a significant part in the total system. Unfortunately, man and machine are not totally compatible. Each contributes special capabilities—the machine such capabilities as precision, power, endurance, and the man such capabilities as judgment, recognition, creativity. The efficiency of the total is often dependent upon the efficiency of the interface between man and machine. This contributes to some of the uncertainty surrounding the management of any organization. While the behavior of the machine may be predicted quite precisely, the behavior of the man may be predicted only in a probabilistic sense.

Uncertainty also exists about the environment beyond the boundaries of the system. The operation of the system must always proceed with incomplete information concerning such external factors as the behavior of competition, govern-

3

ment regulations, technology innovation, and many others. Much of the management concern is centered on the predictions, judgments, and evaluations of these areas of uncertainty. The organizational system, then, operates in an environment of uncertainty, both within and beyond its boundaries.

Management requires information to make more precise estimates of the effects of these uncertainties. The amount of information available to management has increased exponentially in recent years. The electronic computer has provided a practical means to organize and process this flood of information. Rapidly advancing computer technology provides the ability to store and process a mass of data and to rapidly make all types of calculations with increasing accuracy, flexibility, and constantly decreasing cost. The computer has allowed practical advances toward the quantification of meaningful prediction techniques, decision rules, and other management sciences. This computer-generated information has become essential to more sophisticated management methods and in some cases indispensable to the survival of the organization. Therefore, these organizations and their management systems are inevitably tied to the computer.

HISTORY

The use of the computer as a management tool is relatively new. The first real business application of it was probably no earlier than the mid-1950's. Since then the growth has been explosive.

In the late fifties industry approached the computer with a great deal of timidity. The first computer jobs were generally justified purely on the economic grounds of re-

4

ducing clerical work. There was frequently much uncertainty about the probability of success. Therefore the first job selected was repetitive, with a large clerical staff and with well-known and accepted procedures. The next job selected might well be completely unrelated to the first, but with the same factors, except perhaps not so many clerks, and so on. Each job was called an "application."

It is therefore not surprising that most business data-processing installations became very application-oriented. There was an application for payroll, a different application for inventory status, another for customer accounting, cost distribution, sales analysis, and so forth. A great deal of emphasis was put on how to utilize the computer efficiently.

Perhaps not until the early 1960's did many organizations become fully aware of the computer's potential for solving management problems. Here again, as problems were identified and new techniques developed, each became a new application. Production control was an application different from quality control, and each had its own sources of information, terminology, and classification methods. As an organization developed more and more "applications," it found that while solving some problems, it had created several new ones. There was more information available than anyone could digest or evaluate. There were frequently conflicts between the results from two applications; for example, a report on employee absenteeism from the payroll application presented different numbers from the absenteeism rate derived from the personnel application. When the organization attempted to solve problems involving several departments, there was no relationship between the data in the several applications—the decisions in product mix would certainly affect inventory investment, but unfortunately the production control application and the inventory control application did not communicate with each other.

5

Many authorities had recognized this problem and had proposed integrated systems serving several departments within an organization. However, it was not until the mid-1960's that organizations began to recognize the value of information as a basic resource of the organization. They then began to abandon the application-by-application approach and move toward systems which would serve several functions within the organization. The emphasis shifted from reduction of clerical work to such intangible areas as improved decision making and increased efficiency of the organization. Several terms were used—"broader systems" "total systems," and "integrated systems." There were several factors which made these larger systems both desirable and feasible. Certainly, the development of the third generation of computer hardware, with its lower costs and increased flexibility, provided the technological foundation. The increasing acceptance and understanding of the computer as a management tool by all levels of management provided the favorable environment. There are, however, two key factors which seemed to pave the way for the move toward larger, more integrated information systems—the cost of information and the competitive advantages of the system.

First, the information available to and required by management has increased significantly in recent years. At the same time, the reduction of computer cost and the increase in labor costs has made manual tasks a most significant part of the total system cost. Only the integrated system can minimize the cost of data collection and analysis by efficient data management.

Second, these systems not only provide significant reductions in operating costs but also frequently result in outstanding advantages in the services and benefits that can be provided to the customer. Most often, these marketing advantages cannot be reproduced by a competitor without the full system backup.

The larger systems, supported by a greatly improved technological foundation in both computer science and management science, have placed the computer systems directly in the path of the day-to-day management of the organization. This new role of the computer, as an active participant in the management of the organization, is just beginning to emerge. It certainly appears to be the dominant management innovation of the 1970's and one which will accelerate the invasion of the computer into the operation of all types of organizations.

MANAGEMENT INFORMATION SYSTEMS

The management process may be examined from many perspectives. Whatever the definition of management, it always involves the evaluation and communication of information. Information is necessary to formulate objectives and policy which subsequently must be interpreted and communicated to many people. The evaluation of these objectives and the subsequent decisions and action plans are based upon information concerning their impact on the organization. Plans and schedules must be communicated to those responsible for action. Control is achieved only when actions are fed back to management for evaluation and the alteration of future plans.

Management in its many roles must be cognizant of its environment before it may effectively fulfill its function in the organization. This requires knowledge of its own internal productive resources—facilities, manpower, inventories, money, etc. It also requires knowledge of external factors—

7

competition, markets, regulations, etc. If this information is incomplete or inaccurate, it can be a limiting factor upon the efficiency of management. But even further, there must be a mechanism to correlate and evaluate this information and to predict the consequences of proposed actions. The objective of the information system is to make available a broad base of comprehensive, accurate information. The concept of the management system is the provision of an orderly, systematic method of controlling and directing this vital management resource—information.

The systems required by various types of organizations will certainly differ in form and content—the specific capabilities of a hospital system will be different from a manufacturing system or banking system—just as the solution to their management problems will differ. Even within a single industry, comparable organizations will devise different systems to meet their unique management philosophies and objectives. There are, however, basic characteristics that will apply to all types of organizations.

One of the basic principles underlying the concept of management information in all organizations is the treatment of information as a basic resource of the organization. Most of the information available to any organization will be of interest to several departments and will be used in the many functions of management. A given element of data will be summarized and transformed into many types of measures and statistics. This information will be employed for many purposes at many times. The management information system strives to collect every fact of interest to the organization in an accurate, efficient manner. The system may then use these data to provide comprehensive and meaningful information to all departments and functions.

With this pool of information the system is able to aid in the coordination of the many organizational activities.

The availability of accurate and standardized data will provide the basis for the automation of routine communication and decision functions. This capability provides the second general characteristic of the management information system—the ability to integrate the operations both vertically and laterally. The detailed facts related to work assignments and production accomplishments are essential to scheduling, but they retain their value as they are summarized for production control administration. In a similar manner the same facts will be used to provide realistic planning and evaluation by higher levels of management. With consistent information each succeeding function can relate and communicate in a meaningful manner. Consistency and standardization of information are equally important in lateral coordination. The production schedule is meaningful to such functions as inventory and sales only when both can relate to a common denominator, such as a part number. The common information resource not only allows for the automation of routine decisions, both laterally and vertically, but equally important it will cause all other decision processes to be more efficient and more responsive to the real-time needs of the organization simply by virtue of improved information.

Management information is intrinsically linked with the computer because of its data-processing power. But a characteristic of the management information system is recognition of the interaction of man and machine in the total environment of organizational management. The assignment of specific roles to man or to machine will vary with the nature of the organization and the sophistication of the system. The objective of the system concept is optimization of the total system, which is a combination of people and computers. It is no longer sufficient to use a computer effectively. Rather, it is necessary to provide efficient interfaces between man and machine so that the total system operates in a reliable and efficient manner. The system initates action on the part of men and facilities through the interpretation and display of information. It achieves control by receiving facts concerning the actions and decisions made as a result of this information. The true management system encompasses an effective two-way communication between people and computer.

The development of the management information system must, then, draw upon the methodologies and techniques of many disciplines to provide these diverse capabilities. This fusing of several disciplines is one reason that these systems have scope and capabilities beyond prior business uses of the computer. Any of the conventional disciplines, such as accounting, marketing, engineering, and operations, may be found in the development and operation of the management information system. There are, however, three major disciplines that are always present to some degree in the development of these systems.

Computer Technology—The electronic computer supplies the foundation of the system with its ability to process large volumes of data quickly and efficiently.

Management Sciences—The computer system can process more information than people can use. Analytical and statistical techniques must reduce this volume to meaningful form and content.

Systems Analysis—Management involves a complex interrelationship of men, machines, and functions. Systems science allows those elements to be efficiently integrated into the total operation.

LIMITATIONS

Although the larger management information systems are becoming increasingly beneficial, in some cases even essential, to the management of the organization, the very things that make them so attractive have also made them difficult to design and implement. These systems are expensive both in terms of people needed to develop them and in terms of the computer hardware needed to support them. Unfortunately, they also have had a tendency to cost more and require more time than estimated. The systems rapidly become obsolete with changing management objectives, competitive environments, and technological advances, and it can be difficult and expensive to improve these systems once they are installed. As the organization becomes more dependent on the system, the problems of accuracy and reliability become critical. A major system failure can have disastrous effects on the organization. Man and machine are not always a compatible combination. The rigid machine discipline can conflict with human behavior. The computer's command of information resources can cause extensive and sometimes painful and unexpected realignments of organizational structure.

The design of the management system must not only provide the obvious advantages, but equally important, it must also preclude the potentially dangerous effects of such systems. Management systems can become so rigid that changes or improvements are difficult and expensive. This may inhibit or postpone vital innovations in operations or management. It may even disguise the need for such changes. Similarly, rigid systems may tend to discourage and conceal areas where human ingenuity and creativity can achieve substantial benefits over formal decision rules. Formal decision

11

rules are always based on imperfect mathematical models while the human being can recognize complex patterns and exceptions with great proficiency. The more comprehensive the computer portion of the system, the greater the danger, for much of the actual mechanics of the operation may be hidden deep within the unfeeling computer. The design of the management system must be concerned with these dangers if the system is to achieve its full potential. The system design should promote rather than discourage the human capabilities of judgment and decision making. It should facilitate the recognition, evaluation, and implementation of new policies and procedures. It must be as dynamic in form and concept as is the organization it is to serve.

2

Design Considerations

THE COMPUTER has been successfully utilized by many types of organizations for a number of years. There have been payroll systems, accounting systems, inventory systems, and similar systems in which administrative chores have been assigned to the computer. Equally significant has been the application of management science techniques such as optimization and simulation of organizational planning and decision-making, techniques which would have been impractical without the computational speed of the digital computer.

Even with this background, the current emphasis centers on several new areas—areas such as total systems, online systems, integrated systems, and so on. All of these terms seem to be equated to another new area, management information systems, and all signify a whole new approach to the use of the computer. This new approach cannot be one of technical revolution, for the current principles of computer science have been present for some time. Large-scale real-time business systems date back to the late 1950's, when American Airlines conceived its SABRE reservations sys-

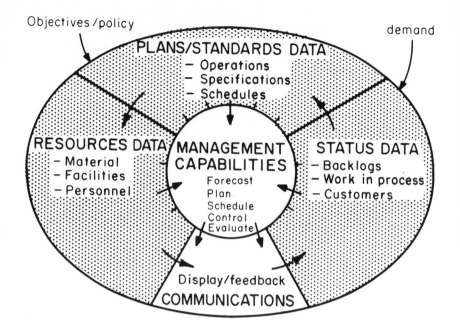

Figure 2.1. Management information system data base relationship

tem. The difference in the current approach must then be a philosophical difference, a recognition of broader management objectives and of greater potential in the use of the computer. There are two areas of emphasis that typify this new approach.

Total System—There is a continuing move to develop systems which interface the many functions within the organization. Even more significant is the recognition of the interface between the individual and the computer—the man and machine interface. It is no longer necessary or sufficient to maximize the efficiency of the computer or of a single department. The concern is the optimum operation of the total organization.

14

Decision Process—The total system—the man and machine system—is becoming increasingly involved in the actual decision-making process. It is no longer a research tool or a bookkeeping machine. The system is becoming a vital part of the day-to-day operation and management of the organization.

Many computer-based management systems employing these principles have been designed and installed during the past several years. Not all have been completely successful. The key to success is not just the development of online systems or the merging of several systems into one large system. The key is the development of systems which serve more of the real needs of management and do so more efficiently than a series of individual systems. In meeting these objectives, there have been many problems. The major causes, however, seem to fall into two categories.

Obsolescence—After the management systems have been installed, they have been difficult and expensive to modify or improve. Business is a dynamic institution and is constantly changing. The management systems have often been unable to keep pace with changes in the organization. Therefore, the system rapidly becomes obsolete and is no longer responsive to the needs of the organization.

Development Schedules—The development has been difficult to manage, for it has frequently required much more time, effort, and cost than had been expected. Potential problems are not isolated early enough to preclude schedule delays.

Both of these difficulties emphasize the fact that the organizational use of the computer is no longer primarily a technical problem. The problems are primarily ones of management—how to determine management needs and then how to manage the systems planning and the systems design to meet these needs. (The problems of systems management

15

will be covered in Chapter 3 and Chapter 4.) This chapter will provide an overview of some of the design considerations essential to the development of management systems which achieve organizational objectives and provide continuing support to these objectives.

SYSTEM OBJECTIVES

Management information systems are being developed for a variety of organizations. They cover such diverse institutions as transportation companies, banks, hospitals, brokerage firms, manufacturing concerns, government, retail sales organizations, and schools. The management systems for each organization have a different emphasis and architecture. Even within a class of organizations or among the individual departments of a single organization, there will be unique features.

However, even though the architecture differs in each case, there are many similarities in both system objectives and the approaches used to develop the system. This commonality is expressed in the growing body of knowledge used to define, study, and evaluate these systems. The methods are generally referred to as systems analysis, and the approach is referred to as the systems concept. From these two areas emerge principles that apply to all the systems that men develop to manage the complex organizations that they conceive.

The terms "systems concept" and "systems approach," which have become popular in recent years, are a way of viewing any organization of physical or human components. This view expands the examination of any operation to include all other operations which influence the behavior of the operation under study. As all operations have some impact on other operations, which have impact on other operations, and so on, this view could cause the examination of any operation to include the entire universe. Obviously this is impractical. From a practical point of view, what the system concept does imply is consideration of the organization in as broad a context as possible. The optimization of an individual operation or department will not necessarily optimize the total organization. There are, however, points where the potential impact of the interaction will diminish below the threshold values of the impact of additional investigation. These tradeoff considerations will define practical boundaries for the system. When these system boundaries have been established, the system concept requires that all the chain effects of the relationships within these boundaries be considered.

The system concept leads to several design objectives or design principles that apply to all management information systems. Perhaps the most apparent is the move to a larger system. The functional systems, such as accounting, inventory, marketing, operations, and so on, have been engulfed by the larger systems. When the larger systems tend to include several functions (or departments), they are referred to as integrated systems. The advantage of the larger systems is not that several functional requirements have been brought together but rather that the larger systems meet the needs of the several functions more completely and more efficiently than the individual systems.

There is also a greater emphasis placed on the interaction between the man and the computer—the man and machine interface. In most early uses of the computer, the objective was to have the computer accomplish the tedious calculations involved in many business functions. As such, the concern was to develop the maximum computer efficiency. Today the concern is the total efficiency of the man and computer combination. The objective is to present the results

17

of the calculation to people in a way that maximizes the efficiency of the total man and machine system. At the same time there is a move to use the system—the man and machine system—in the decision-making process. Formal systems are becoming concerned with problems involving unknowns, predictions, and judgments. The computer system is no longer in a research or an advisory capacity. It is no longer a bookkeeping machine which periodically prints past data. The immense amounts of data generated by corporate record keeping can be captured as it is created and can be used to construct memory banks. Rapid access to these data, coupled with the computer's computational power, provides support in many types of decision areas. The computer system is becoming part of the day-to-day operation of the organization.

The view of the organization as a system has also revealed the rather universal nature of information. As mentioned in Chapter 1, most facts related to the organization will be used by several departments and management levels and in several time frames. The conservation and proper management of information are fundamental requirements of the system. Two prime elements in this task are the economical collection of data and the efficient storage of information.

ACTIVITY REPORTING

The reporting of operating activity is the substance of any information system. Decision making must proceed from an evaluation of the current operational environment. This decision making is limited not only by the validity of the technique employed but even more fundamentally by the validity of the data used to make the decision. The method and policies used to acquire the basic data are major factors in the usefulness of the total system.

Data collection is also one of the most expensive aspects of any information system. Considerable amounts of time and effort are required by both people and the computer in providing data to the system. The design effort directed toward collecting data with maximum usefulness at a minimum cost is most worthwhile.

To be useful, the data must be accurate, timely, and meaningful. Accuracy, of course, is never absolute. However, the system must be designed and controlled to provide acceptable accuracy levels. Before information can serve a control function, its acquisition must precede the time that action is to be taken. To be meaningful, the data must relate to the real world in a precise and predictable manner.

DATA BASE

All organizations are required to maintain ever-increasing amounts of information. Some of this information is basically historical and is used to meet legal, regulatory, and management control requirements. Other elements of information are required for operations management and include the current status of such resources as inventory, employees, work in process, open orders, and facilities. All of this information must be systematically managed by the system so that it will be available when needed.

Most of this information will be required at several times by several departments in varying forms. For example, in manufacturing, the status of work in process on the production floor could provide information at different times and in different forms to such departments as inventory control, production control, and cost accounting, to mention a few. This commonality of requirements has led to the principle of single-source files. Each element of basic information is collected once and stored in one place. All users go to this

19

single source for the information they require. This concept is often called a data bank or data base.

The data base has many advantages. Immediately apparent is the potential reduction in data-collection effort and required storage capacity, as each fact must be recorded and stored only once. Equally significant is the very real potential of more accurate, more comprehensive, and more current data. This potential, unfortunately, is somewhat offset by the rigorous and sophisticated design effort required by a database installation.

THE IMPACT OF CHANGE

The business organization is a dynamic complex. It is constantly changing to meet changes in its external and internal environment. External environment may change as a result of such things as competitive maneuvers or government policy. The internal environment can be just as dynamic. The production process is subject to constant technological changes. Management techniques themselves are a rapidly developing science and contribute constant changes to the management policies and strategies.

The information system itself must be able to change with these changes in the organization. As the system becomes a more and more integrated part of the management process, it may well dictate, to a large degree, the ability of the organization to utilize technological advances in any field. The management information system contributes to the generation of these changes by providing better decision making, but it must do more; the information system must aid in the implementation of these changes even when they are changes in the system itself. The design objectives then must include both flexibility and adaptability. Flexibility is the ability of the system to manage a wide variety of circumstances as it is designed. Adaptability is the ability to meet major changes in environment with a minimum of modifications.

One of the best ways to preclude obsolescence of the information system is to assure that the basic structure follows the fundamental nature of the organization. Data-collection and data-base structure should be at a fundamental level. This basic structure is the most difficult and expensive part of the system to change. In general, these programs must be complex and highly integrated to be efficient, and therefore they are difficult to change. They involve understanding and use by many people, and therefore modifications can involve extensive retraining programs and in-process conversions. With a solid basic structure it is relatively simple to change routine control reports or to make special reports or studies. Where the information is available, the data-reduction and data-computations programs can be modified or new ones added without extensive impact on other programs or on operating personnel.

Programs that involve policy statements or mathematical models representing operational philosophy are the most subject to change. Advances in management science are constantly making existing rules and policies obsolete. For the information system to be the most beneficial to management, it must be able to absorb and to implement these new rules and policies quickly and inexpensively. Generally, a complete system should not be built around one specific policy. The programs for calculations and decision rules should be built in modular form, so that only one module contains the specific policy or operational model. Then when a modification is required, only the new module need be programmed and installed.

A part of the evaluation of any design is its economic aspect. To build flexibility into the system may increase the cost of the system. The benefits are chiefly intangible but are significant. The following general factors should be considered in reviewing the design of the management information system:

1. It is virtually certain that there will be changes in the organization during the life cycle of the system even though specific changes cannot be predicted.

2. A part of the cost of maintaining the organization is the cost of maintaining the information system, whether it is formal or informal.

3. One of the very real economic benefits of an information system is the ability it provides management to rapidly and efficiently implement decisions concerning policy and procedure changes.

SUMMARY

The design of larger integrated management information systems must provide both operating efficiency and the ability to adapt to inevitable changes of the organizational environment within which it must survive. Several design considerations are the key to success in both areas. Such factors as the analysis of information flow, modular design, the efficient collection and storage of data—all interact to establish the operating characteristics of the system. Each of these areas will be treated in subsequent chapters to define its contribution to the whole.

However, the approach to managing the design task itself must provide assurance that the system will not only meet its operating objectives but will also meet time and cost targets. Because much of the actual design is set by management philosophy and organization of the system design effort, the next two chapters discuss some aspects of this problem and establish a framework for the subsequent discussion of design techniques.

3

System Life Cycle

ONLY ONE FACET of computer-oriented management information system seems to meet with general agreement. This might be summarized by the common observation that information systems invariably cost more than expected and are seldom operational on schedule. The management problems in achieving cost and schedule goals for developing information systems would not appear to be inherently more difficult than those experienced with any other project; however, as industry moves from smaller data-processing projects to larger, more complex information systems, the problem becomes more acute.

Perhaps part of the problem is the relative lack of experience with the concept of a total system. This can cause many of the time-consuming and risk-prone aspects of these systems to be underestimated or even unrecognized. Or perhaps the problem is that when compared to physical systems, the products of management systems are primarily ideas, objectives, policies, and similar concepts, which are difficult to describe and define. Consequently, it is difficult to define

23

checkpoints or milestones by which management may evaluate and control the project development. Either of these problems can be solved, however, if the total life cycle of the management system can be anticipated at the outset of the project.

In the larger, more integrated management systems, the steps in the development cycle are quite different from those that have conventionally been associated with data-processing operations. The conventional approaches tend to allow the data aspects of the problem to overshadow the decision aspects. The management system therefore seems to have development problems more nearly related to those of physical

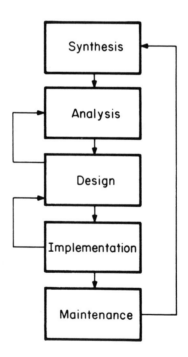

Figure 3.1. System life cycle

systems. The difference in management systems, as already mentioned, lies primarily in the difficulty in defining milestones where physical products are not present. In an effort to describe the development cycle of management systems, five steps have been isolated. These steps are in general terms so they may fit the variety of situations encountered, but it is to be hoped that they are specific enough to allow effective planning and control. Within each step it is possible to define the activities which may occur. These activities may occur in several sequences but, nevertheless, must be completed during that step in the development of any management information system. The five steps are:

1. Synthesis—The rather general need which originated the project could be solved in many ways. The first step is to develop a concept with specific objectives and boundaries.

2. Analysis—The system concept will be subject to detailed evaluation to determine the best methods to achieve the objective, and these methods will be defined.

3. Design and Documentation—The results of analysis will be expanded into a detailed design, and these design details will be recorded.

4. Implementation—The individual elements of the detailed design will be integrated and collectively tested, and the system will be placed in operation.

5. Maintenance—The useful operating life of the system will cover several years and will require maintenance, modification, and improvements.

The impetus for a system may originate in a variety of ways. Management objectives or priorities may indicate the need for improved formal systems. Long-range organizational goals or competitive influences may establish the need. Regardless of how the idea is originated, a great deal of effort and a variety of skills must be deployed in a coordinated manner before a usable product is produced. The first step will be an examination of the original impetus itself.

SYNTHESIS

Synthesis involves the investigation of many generally related subjects and the evaluation of several different approaches to the problems. It may also involve the review of fundamental objectives and policies of the organization. A study of existing knowledge of the organization as it may be displayed in existing operating procedures, policies, and systems may also be involved. From this welter of facts the system designers must create a unified concept on which the system can be built. To define the system concept in terms of both form and scope, the designer must consider many things, including the environment in which the system is to operate, the relationship to other existing or planned systems—really the relation to total organization, the real needs of the organization, and the relationship of the system to the long-range plans or strategies of the organization and the value to the organization of the system.

This is, to a large degree, a problem of information retrieval. A system of any size will require many specialized talents (knowledge), in such fields as accounting, engineering, personnel, mathematics, and others. There are several techniques that may be used to obtain this information. Interviews and discussions with operating management will define objections, missions, and problems. Studies of similar systems will show how other organizations have solved the problems. Much of the necessary information, however, is not available in recognizable form. It must be "created" through the knowledge and experience of the designers. Therefore informal meetings, even "brainstorming" sessions, are characteristic at this point. In general, the investigators will assume that anything can be done if it is necessary. The solution may even involve pure research.

As a picture of needs and possible solutions develops, decisions must be made concerning the scope of the program. This will include boundaries, time constraints, man-machine responsibilities, implementation plan, and resources required, in terms of men, machines, and money. At some point the proposed system must be reduced to broad specifications. The objectives must be defined, and the broad methods of achieving the objectives must be outlined. The general specifications may include input-output requirements and volumes. Response times and the man-machine interfaces must be defined. There should also be an estimate of the decision rules that must be developed and the data-processing capacities required.

When the general specifications have been completed, there can be an initial evaluation of the technical and economic feasibility of the system. The evaluation will include such factors as:

Resources Required—The required resources include the people and talent for design, programming, and implementation: the computer and other hardware requirements; and the management time and talent required for implementations and conversions. These factors will show the total financial resources that must be provided over the system life cycle in addition to the technical talent which must be made available.

Value to the Organization—While the value of the system may generally be thought of in economic terms, it may also lie in largely intangible areas, and it even may be mandatory to the continued success of the organization.

27

Probability of Success—The feasibility of the program frequently must be expressed in probabilistic terms. Consideration should be given to time constraints and the probability of meeting deadlines. The research and development requirements should be evaluated in terms of the risks involved. The probability that the system can meet reliability and performance crieria must be assessed.

It should be noted that while a great deal of technical and management skills will be ultimately involved with the system, the decisions and tradeoffs made at this point will limit the eventual value of the system both in terms of overall value and in terms of feasibility and practicability.

Once a basic design concept has been developed and evaluated, the next two steps are generally management approval and a development plan, although not necessarily in that order. Management approval is almost always required at this point. Even where a formal approval is not specifically required, it is generally necessary to brief management at several levels on how the original objective is to be achieved. Many of the subsequent steps will require a great deal of management support. During this phase meetings with management will not only provide feedback on the sufficiency of design concepts but will also provide much of the necessary support through an appreciation of the system.

The development plan is essential to the subsequent management of the program. The long lead-time development projects must be identified. There may be many people from different organizations required to design and implement the system; special skills and talents must be identified so they may be allocated to the program. Coordination and interface problems must be described, and critical decision points defined. The specific factors to be considered will depend upon the nature and scope of the project but will probably include procurement of special or additional computer hardware, assignment of analysts to specialized areas, programmer work loads, development of mathematical models, preparation of facilities, training of personnel, devising of the testing program, building of major files, and working out of the conversion and implementation plan.

The initial phase can generally be considered complete when three things are present: (1) preliminary specifications to the depth that detailed design may proceed; (2) a plan for the design and implementation of the system; and (3) approval by management of the concept and the allocation of resources to the development plan.

ANALYSIS

During the analysis phase the techniques and methods required to accomplish the objectives defined in the synthesis phase will be developed. For each task there may be several alternate methods proposed, and in this phase each of these must be evaluated. These evaluations will be logical in nature and will include consideration of economy, efficiency, feasibility, and accuracy. The analysis phase might be termed "looking for trouble," whereas in the synthesis phase everything was considered possible. Each element within the system must be scrutinized for potential operating problems. Every possible error in logic must be exposed, missing links in flow must be identified, inefficiency or inadequacy in input or output methods must be corrected.

The techniques and tools used by the designer will, of course, depend on the specific nature of the problem. Flowcharting is a standard method of representing material or information flow and is a standard tool of computer-oriented designers. The tools of cost accounting, operations research, engineering economy, methods engineering, and re-

29

lated disciplines will be used where appropriate. One area that should be given careful consideration is all the man-machine interfaces. The instances where operating personnel must provide inputs to the system or use outputs from the system are the point in the system where the most potential problems exist.

At this time standard practices for design and operation of the system will be developed if they are not already available. They will include such items as standard coding and classification systems, standard output formats, standard definitions, standard abbreviations, and standard terminology. Technical standards such as data transfer and handling, programming languages, programming conventions and similar matters should be defined.

The operational life of the system is an important consideration during this phase. It is almost certain that the organization will experience conditions and needs during the life of the system that cannot be anticipated during its development. Much of the value of the system will relate to its ability to satisfy these changing needs. When designed, the system should be as flexible in meeting changing environments as is economically practical.

In addition, the basic structure should have the capacity to adapt to modification and improvement as advances in technology and management practice become available. These capabilities may be achieved through modular design, selection of fundamental data sources, and sound design of basic files. Whatever the specifics of the individual system, its flexibility and adaptability are key considerations.

For a system of any complexity, the design problem of minimizing potential failures and errors is quite difficult. Major problems can develop where several people and/or groups are working on a project. Discrepancies in interface specification can easily develop. Open areas and omissions can develop if subsystem boundaries are misunderstood. There are several ways to ensure design compatibility.

Rigorous Standards—Of course, absolute standards are expensive, time consuming, and practically impossible when concurrent design is practiced.

Design Review—Periodic reviews of the design as work progresses can identify problems at an early point, before correction becomes expensive. The review group must consist of knowledgeable individuals representing all design groups and disciplines.

Simulation—Design concepts and system parameters can be tested by simulation in several ways. A model system can be set up and actively operated in a limited area with the results compared with predictions, a breadboard type of approach. Where this is not possible, a more abstract mathematical model may be established and the operation simulated by a computer manipulation of synthetic data. The problem with any type of simulation is that the complexity of establishing the model may rival the complexity of the system itself.

The participation of operating management in the design decisions in the analysis phase can provide valuable assistance. The operating management can supply the specifics of the environment in which the system will operate. Their participation will also provide them with an understanding of the system objectives and methods that will promote a commitment to the system, thereby easing the problems inherent in the transition to the new system during the implementation phase.

The completion of the analysis phase will usually include several rather detailed specifications. The documents will usually include system flow charts, file designs and layouts, input data elements, formats for primary output, formulas

31

for calculations, and performance and timing specifications.

At this point another evaluation probably will be (or should be) made of the entire system. Is it economically justified? Is it technically feasible? Does it achieve the objectives? When this reevaluation is successfully passed, the plan may again be submitted for management approval. While this approval may be informal or formal, it should be remembered that this is probably the last chance for management to reevaluate its original objective and its decision to proceed with this project. From this point on, projects have a tendency to continue indefinitely on a self-perpetuating basis without an opportunity for reevaluation. If business conditions have changed or if the original decision was marginal, the project should be canceled at this time, before additional resources are committed.

The analysis phase therefore should result in (1) assurance of technical feasibility, (2) decision on methods, techniques, and equipment, (3) system specifications, and (4) approval to proceed.

DESIGN AND DOCUMENTATION

After the analysis is completed, there remains a great amount of detail which must be developed and recorded. During this phase a variety of people will generally be working on a variety of projects. Scheduling and coordination problems may be difficult.

The documentation aspect of this phase cannot be overemphasized. During the life of the system there will be many times when it will be necessary to refer to this detail. Many of the problems that will be discovered during testing can be analyzed only with reference to the detail. Even after implementation there will be operational problems which must be isolated and resolved. During the operating life of the system there will be situations which demand design changes. There may be times when it is necessary to modify or improve the system. It may be desirable to substitute equipment as new technical tools become available. As the business environment changes, it may be necessary to expand the system in either capabilities or coverage. New people will become involved in the system in both maintenance and operation. If adequate documentation is not available, it may become necessary to "redesign" the system to discover the proper interfaces for the modifications.

The design work will vary with specific systems. However, the following categories will generally be present in any system to some degree.

Computer Programs—The computer program is essentially a procedure, and properly annotated, it can be quite informative. Computer programs are usually accompanied by detailed flow charts or decision tables. These forms of documentation are essential for both maintenance and any later modifications or improvements.

Equipment and Facilities Layout—Because most of the equipment will probably be "off the shelf" procurement, the primary problems are equipment layout, location, and installation of data-collection terminals, transmission cables, and similar requirements.

Manuals and Procedures—The people who are to operate the system will require specific operating procedures. These are usually published in a manual which includes such items as rules and policy, forms and transcripts, operating instructions for data-collection devices and/or other equipment, error correction, and emergency procedures. Operational aids, such as quick references, checklists, and similar devices, may also be quite useful.

33

Computer Operating Procedures—Operating procedures will vary greatly, depending on the equipment configurations and data-collection media. They should, however, cover whatever is necessary for normal computer operations, operating schedules, data-handling procedures, and any required emergency and failure recovery procedures.

Training Material and Programs—The general requirements for training are developed during the analysis phase. Training material and program details will be required both for personnel who will operate the system and for management people who will use the system in their decision process. While the two groups may require different training approaches, any approach may use a variety of media—for example, written material and various classroom and audiovisual aids.

The design phase completion should include (1) computer programs which have been individually tested and debugged, (2) operating procedures for all areas with system operating responsibilities (3) complete documentation of programs, procedures, and equipment, and (4) training program for both operating personnel and management.

IMPLEMENTATION

System implementation is one of the most difficult aspects of the system cycle. Coordination is required with the designers and all operating departments. Problems will invariably occur in unpredictable fashions. The implementation team must be staffed and organized to recognize and correct these problems. Schedule slippages are classic in this phase and can be prevented only by reasonable schedules, effective coordination, and competent management of problems as they occur. During this phase many things must be done, including testing, training, coordination, and implementation.

System testing is a critical step. During design the individual elements will be tested thoroughly—programs will be tested, devices and hardware will be tested, models will be proved. However, only when all the production elements are combined into a system can the system's effectiveness be tested. This must be done in the most precise manner practical. The extent of testing will depend to some degree on the cost or penalty of a failure when the system is in operation. Many methods can be used. The important point is to test the total system in a situation as close to its real environment as possible. It is always easier to make corrections on a system during testing than during operation. In many cases it may be advantageous to use representatives of operating departments to conduct the final testing. This will not only represent the type of management that will actually run the system but will also provide valuable familiarization and training for these people.

In most instances it will be necessary to convert from the existing system to the new system. The method of conversion should have been established during the analysis phase. Exact procedures must be established in this phase and coordinated with the testing and implementation schedules. Two types of conversion are frequently encountered. First, static data files must be converted from an old system to the new system; second, there is in-process conversion, where an operating system is replaced by the new system. The second conversion may involve such things as a complete inventory of a warehouse, the exchanging of all job cards in the shop, the provision of new forms to all employees, and similar actions.

All personnel connected with the system must be trained

35

prior to implementation. There may be different degrees of training for different classes of employees, and the training must be carefully coordinated with testing and implementation schedules. To the greatest extent possible, training should take advantage of things learned during testing. It should also be conducted as near in time to the activation of the system as possible so that effectiveness is not lost.

The implementation phase continues until the new system is in operation and includes (1) a complete test of the system, (2) a training program, (3) conversion to the new system, and (4) generally, the termination of the old system.

MAINTENANCE

The management of the system during its operating life will probably be divided into two phases, the learning curve and routine maintenance. The learning curve will start immediately after implementation of the system and will invariably be laden with problems. The operating personnel will be learning the system and will be making excessive mistakes. Close attention must be given to keep the error rate within design limits. This will require close monitoring, follow-up, and possibly selective retraining. It can generally be expected that there will be failures of equipment and programs during the early life of the system. These should be expected, and provisions should be made to identify and correct problems as quickly as possible. It also can be expected that there will be discrepancies in system logic, especially if the system is large or complex. This type of problem requires early detection and correction.

Most systems will require some attention during their entire life cycle. This routine maintenance will generally fall into the following categories:

1. Random Failures and Problems—Unexpected problems may occur at any time and must be corrected promptly to prevent gradual degeneration of the system performance.

2. Compliance—Whenever there are people involved, the system is subject to noncompliance either through negligence or misinformation. This kind of problem must be monitored constantly so that it remains within control.

3. Improvements—Changing environmental conditions within which the system operates may make it desirable to modify the system in order to improve its operations.

CONCURRENCY

As systems become larger, it is frequently undesirable and often impractical to implement the whole system at one time. The system must be divided into segments for both development and implementation. The use of segments and the principle of concurrent development, as shown in Figure 3.2, can reduce the overall cycle of the total project. It can provide for leveling of work loads within special skills and, of course, can provide benefits from the system at an early date. However, multiple segments will make planning and

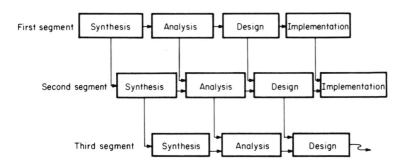

Figure 3.2. Concurrent system development

37

control more complex, and this will frequently require the use of such planning aids as the various network-type techniques. All of these planning requirements place a greater premium on the firm definition of the steps within the life cycle.

Among the problems that can be avoided is that of over-lapping boundaries—two or more implementation segments attempting to cover the same management area. This problem of boundaries relates to interface compatibility. Design steps must be sequenced so that their interrelationship can be defined before critical design phases are committed. Firm definition of the steps within each segment can also prevent errors in simple logic that may slip into a complex multiple-segment phase project.

SUMMARY

As management systems become broader and move toward the total systems concept, they also generally become more sophisticated in that more decision processes are included within the system. Both of these added complexities— size and sophistication—cause development programs that are more difficult to manage. The first step toward improved control of development costs and schedules is recognition of the various steps involved in total cycle (see Figure 3.3 for the five basic steps in the system life cycle). With an understanding of the effort required, each activity within these phases can be given proper consideration when time tables are developed and resources are allocated.

	Synthesis	Analysis	Design	Implementation	Maintenance
Considerations	•Definition of project •Alternate approaches •Scope of project •Value of project	•Evolution of methods •Mathematical models •Equipment configuration •Data requirements	•Programs and documentation •Manuals and procedures •Equipment specifications and layout •Training methods	•Coordination of conversions •Correction of test problems •Training schedules	•Equipment failures •Personnel errors •System logic problems
Results	•Preliminary specifications •Development plan •Management approval	•Assurance of feasibility •Methods and techniques •System specifications •Approval to proceed	•Operating procedures •Computer programs •Documentation of procedures programs and equipment •Training program	•Tested system •Trained personnel •Conversion to new system •Termination of old system	•Correction of problems •Monitoring of compliance •System improvements

Figure 3.3. Summary of the system life cycle

4

Systems Management

COMPUTERIZED management information systems have created as great a revolution in applied management techniques
as the third-generation computers did in data-processing
techniques. These systems have forced operating management
into direct contact with information-processing technology, an
area which has only recently started to reveal the results of
its own technological explosion. These results are creating
a new maturity in the industry, and with this maturity has
come a marked degree of specialization. There are systems
analysts, programmers, systems engineers, software programmers, computer operators, and a myriad of other professionals.
The undisciplined interaction of this increasing number of
computer specialists with the increasing involvement of the
management generalist has contributed to the chaos which
has surrounded many of the attempts to develop large-scale
management information systems. The resulting misunderstanding has contributed significantly to the problems of managing development costs and schedules.

THE NEED FOR ORGANIZATION

The problem is to provide a bridge from the general perspective of the manager to the increasing specialization in both information and management science technology. At first, this seems identical to the project management problems that must be faced when engineering large-scale physical systems. There is a similarity, but there is also a major difference: The computer system is becoming a part of the management process itself, not a product to be managed.

There is, therefore, a greater need during the design of management information systems to develop a link between the information specialist and the management generalist while providing for efficient utilization of skilled specialists. The magnitude and nature of the problem may vary with the size of the organization; however, the management objectives in any case are the same:

1. Provide information systems that meet the real management needs of the organization.

2. Maintain control of system costs and activation schedules, retaining the ability to respond rapidly to the changing needs of management.

There seems to be no one solution to the problem of organizing for system design. There are several ways to organize, all of which have their place. The proper method or combination of methods will depend on the particular circumstances involved. But before considering the organizational alternatives, we should examine the nature of the function to be performed. This function is the total process of transforming management objectives into operating systems which satisfy those objectives.

SKILL REQUIREMENTS

As mentioned before, the computer has brought with it a series of new job specialities. A brief definition of some of these might be a point at which to start the examination of the design task. These specialties are discussed below.

Systems Analysts

Systems analysts design new systems. They usually start with a problem and design a solution. There is, however, a great difference in the use of the term. At least two types of analysts are widely encountered—the business systems analysts who concentrate primarily upon the system solution and the computer systems analysts who concentrate upon broad technical aspects of utilizing the computer to operate the systems solution.

Operations Research Analysts

Operations research analysts use mathematical techniques to solve business problems. They are closely associated with the computer because the computer first made many of these techniques practical.

Systems Engineers

Systems engineers are concerned with the system as a whole, not just with individual components. They are generally involved with systems where the components are drawn from many fields of science and engineering and are generally concerned with the technical aspects of feedback, control stability, reliability, and other areas of automation. Their

43

general objective is selection of components and systems design which achieve the objective and optimize the system operation.

Programmers

Programmers are the people who convert the rules developed by the analysts into language the computer can understand. They frequently specialize, much as engineers have specialized. Some of the specialists are

Commercial programmers, who work with general business problems, usually use a high-level language and also frequently develop backgrounds in such specific business areas as finance, production, inventory, and so on.

Scientific programmers work with engineering or scientific problems and usually have strong mathematical backgrounds.

Software programmers work with the programs that control and monitor the operation of the computer itself. They work at a fundamental code level and frequently specialize in one family of computer.

Real-time and communication programmers also work closely with the machine and are concerned with the optimum operation of the computer.

Operators

Operators are the people who monitor and supervise the equipment. This includes a variety of jobs which include

Console operators, or computer operators, who monitor the operation of the machine through lights, indicators, and the typewriter at the console. They also perform such functions as the start and stop of programs, load data, and so on.

Keypunch operators use a variety of devices to convert written data to a form that can be used as computer input.

Maintenance personnel are frequently considered part of computer operations; however, they generally are contracted from the computer manufacturer or from a service company.

Machine operators usually run the older punch card equipment, such as sorters, tabulators, and the like, and similar newer equipment, such as optical character readers and other auxiliary equipment on larger computers.

WORK REQUIREMENTS

The development of the management system must pass through a series of more or less sequential steps from the time an objective is determined until a useful system is in operation. This series of steps was outlined in the previous chapter. The life cycle has been expanded somewhat in Figure 4.1. This list illustrates a series of essentially discrete development steps which must be managed to successfully produce a useful system. Examination of this list indicates several differences in the management problems encountered during each of the steps. There are different types of coordination required and different levels of management involved. Different skills and varying degrees of experience are needed, and thus differences in the types of people involved in each step.

The second step in Figure 4.1, the analysis step, illustrates the need for coordinating the activity of several skills. At this time a project may require decision capability in such areas as accounting, inventory control, operation research, and management sciences, in addition to technical data-processing capabilities. There will be a high degree of inter-

Step	Work content	Result
Synthesis	Define management needs and develop concepts to meet those needs	Approved program capable of being implemented
Analysis	Design specific system, including models, data definition, performance requirements, etc.	Preliminary design
Design	Prepare procedures processing specifications, document formats, transcripts, training needs, etc.	System specifications
Programming	Convert specifications into machine instructions	Computer programs
Implementation	Test system, prepare facilities, train, and convert system	Operating system
Maintenance	Moniter operations for understanding, compliance and proper utilization; install system improvements	Achievement of management objectives

Figure 4.1. Steps in system development

change between individual specialties. Management contact will be at a very high level.

When the project moves into the design phase, the same kind of talent may be required. However, the work environment will change. The work assignments can be more specific, and as work objectives are more precise, the supervision can be more direct. Considerably less coordination is probably required and certainly a lower level of management. Therefore within the same specialization considerably less individual competence and experience will be needed than was indicated in the analysis phase. Also, designers tend to specialize within their area of competence and carry their specialties from one project to the next.

The implementation and maintenance of the system require a completely different type of work assignment and skill, that is, a general knowledge of the total system and the organizations as applied to a specific geographical area. Individual men will generally work in a number of short-term assignments. While extensive technical skill may not be required, the individual must recognize problems and arrive at solutions without specific supervisory direction.

These kinds of management problems are summarized in Figure 4.2. A review of this figure should confirm the following observations:

The total cycle is a continual flow. It must have input from the first step to efficiently utilize the subsequent steps. The problem of transfer of information—data, concepts, rules— occurs only when there is a change in method of work assignment.

The primary organizational difference between steps is the method in which work assignments are made and therefore the method in which controls, schedules, and the like can be established.

47

Step	Typical activity	Work methods	Manpower resources
Synthesis	• Determination of needs • Definition of objectives • Tradeoff studies	• Group activity • Interviews • Research	• Organizational background • Creative ability • Management experience
Analysis	• Evaluation of methods • Definition of data • Flow of information	• General assignments • Small groups or individuals • Extensive coordination	• Analytical ability • Mathematical-engineering skill • Limited specialization
Design	• Development of procedures • Design of forms • Creation of training material	• Individual assignments • Specific objectives	• Specialized background or experience • General technical knowledge
Programming	• Designing of flow charts • Coding of program • Testing of program	• Individual assignments • Specific objectives	• Specialized technical training • Specialized experience
Implementation	• Testing of system • Training • In-process conversion	• Small groups or individuals • Specific objectives • Coordination	• General system knowledge • Personal initiative • Verbal and written communication
Maintenance	• Monitoring for compliance • Troubleshooting • Improvements of system	• Individual assignments • Short term projects • Self initiated projects	• Overall system knowledge • Personal initiative • Verbal and written communication

Figure 4.2. Systems development work methods

A key problem is the management of manpower resources—skills, talents, experience, and so on.

One pertinent omission in Figure 4.2 is the specific nature of the skills required. However, even though the types of specialization will vary with the project, they will generally be quite different in each step, even in the same project. Therefore, the management problem of organization will be quite similar, regardless of the nature of the project. These organizational objectives can be summarized as efficient utilization of the multiple manpower and skill resources required and continuity and control of work assignments within each step in the development cycle.

It is generally necessary to provide some type of project management within any systems organization to plan and control the total systems effort. Conversely, there is also a need to provide skilled management to plan, supervise, and control the various skill pools.

MANAGEMENT DIRECTION

For any form of project management to be successful, it must receive the support of top operating management. Project management must report at a level such that it may cross departmental lines and represent top management in changing work methods and organizational responsibility. In addition to the support of top management, it is generally considered essential that top management participate in both the design and implementation of a computer-based information system. They may assist in such areas as (1) defining objectives and goals, (2) maintaining interdepartmental coordination and resolving conflicts, and (3) approving design concepts and capital expenditures.

49

Frequently, a planning committee will be established to coordinate the development and use of these systems. This planning committee should be composed of the top people of all the departments involved. For example, if a system is to cover one plant, the plant manager and his immediate staff might be the planning committee. The committee would therefore represent a level of management within the company where most decisions can be made without being subject to higher review.

One of the best ways to ensure acceptance and use of the new system is to inform all levels of management and operating people of the system status as it is developed. This should start as soon as there are broad concepts to discuss and continue through implementation. The planning committee is an excellent place to start the flow of this information.

PROJECT MANAGEMENT

There are several difficult design management problems associated with even a system of minor complexity. There are many tasks which require scheduling, coordination, and control. There is a variety of specialized skills and talents required at different times during the development cycle. In addition, there is the necessity to develop management participation, understanding, and approval. These management requirements may place conflicting demands on the organization of the system effort. The organizational structure which provides the maximum control of objectives and schedules may be inefficient in the management of the manpower resources. Several organizational approaches are used. One approach is the project team.

The project team concept is a rather recent one in industry and has been used successfully in solving a wide variety of problems. In a project team a small group of people representing a variety of skills or specialties concentrates on a specific problem. This interdisciplinary team then attacks the problem collectively, each contributing to all aspects. This effectively brings on a multitude of viewpoints and technical skills to collectively examine a problem. Frequently, this group is assigned full time to the project and meets more or less continually. This approach can be especially successful in the concept or synthesis stage to develop unique solutions to complex problems. It also can be carried over into later phases to coordinate the design and implementation. Specific design tasks can be assigned to existing departments within the organization, or the design team can be staffed to provide part or all of the design skills required. This type of organization is illustrated in Figure 4.3.

Another approach is that of project manager, or project leader. In this organizational concept, the project leader is assigned the responsibility for coordinating the activities of the several organizations representing the skills necessary to develop the program. This type of organization is shown in Figure 4.4. The project leader must establish objectives,

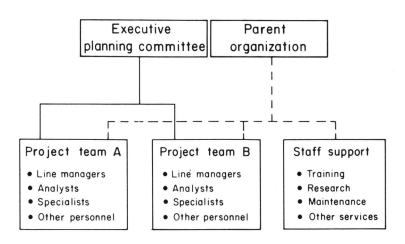

Figure 4.3. Project team organization

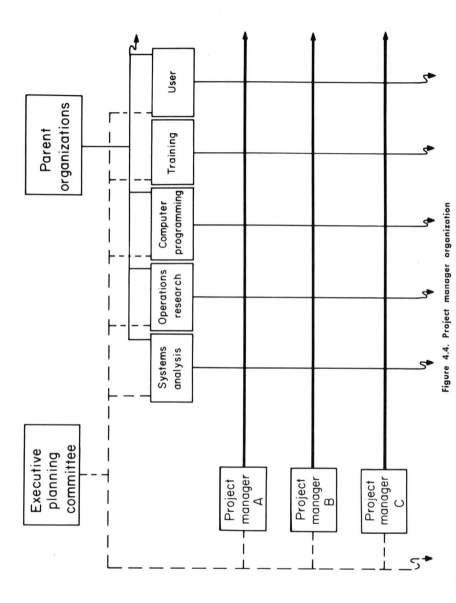

Figure 4.4. Project manager organization

schedules, and deadlines and provide the necessary coordination between the various groups to assure compatibility of the end product. The project leader draws on conventionally organized groups for development and design work. The organization of these design groups is generally such that like skills are grouped together for better utilization of manpower and for supervisory control of work assignments and schedules. The programming staff is usually a group closely associated organizationally with the computer operations organization. Within the systems group there may be specialists in various functional areas, such as cost accounting, industrial engineering, and operations research, or these skills may be drawn from the existing organization when they are required.

Either of the above techniques, a project leader or a project team, will provide coordination and control of multiple tasks but will not provide the proper management of skills. The skills management problem is one of providing the proper skills when needed to meet design schedules, but at the same time leveling work loads so that a consistent work force may be maintained. It is also desirable to maintain continuity of work assignments utilizing individual experience and specialization. The project team may have members with skills which are not required at all times and therefore not fully utilized. It is also difficult to maintain continuity of work specialty from one project to the next. While the project manager will eliminate some of these problems, the process can introduce its own problems of schedule and control. Competing demands from several project managers upon one design group can inflict serious fluctuation on their work load. This results in priority conflicts which can impede the ability of the project leader to control system content, cost, and schedules.

There are, therefore, several reasons why conventional organizations will not always provide the best results when

53

designing management systems. Several organizational tools have been suggested, which include the executive planning committee, the project leader, and the design team. Each tool has its own merit. Conversely, each cannot be advantageously applied to all projects and all organizations. Nor can each tool be applied equally well to all design steps in the development cycle. This suggests that most circumstances can best be handled by a hybrid organization tailored to the needs of the specific circumstance. The key application criterion is the use of only one tool with each definable development step, thus minimizing communication and coordination problems. It will also provide better control over work assignments and, consequently, completion schedules. A hybrid organization might include a design team for the synthesis and analysis steps while a project manager could be assigned for design through implementation.

SUMMARY

There seems to be no "off the shelf" answer to the questions of who should design the computer-oriented management systems. It seems fairly obvious that even in quite small organizations there will be several departments and a variety of individuals involved. Each company and each project will be somewhat different. However, it is imperative that the relationship of the organizations and individuals be designed as finely and thoughtfully as any other part of the program. Whatever the organization, it should provide direction from top management, free flow of ideas and information within the design staff, representation of all operating departments, effective transfer of information between design steps, control and coordination of all work assignments and schedules, and efficient utilization of specialized skills.

5

System Concept

As was mentioned in Chapter 1, the word "system" is widely used in contemporary vocabulary to describe many things in different fields—transportation systems, telephone systems, paperwork systems, weapons systems, computer systems, social systems, nervous systems, judicial systems. The only common characteristic is that each is composed of many different parts and in each case it is the sum of all parts that is of interest. The concept of an orderly collection of a series of different parts implies other characteristics which are usually associated with a system. These characteristics may be generalized as follows:

Coordinated Components—A system is composed of a series of interrelated components or elements whose activities are coordinated according to some set of predetermined rules.

Internal and External Environment—The system concept involves both an external and internal environment. The internal environment is controlled and altered by the interaction of the system components; the external environment consists of forces that act on the system but which are beyond the direct control of the system itself.

Information Flow—A system involves information flow. The coordinated action of the various components, which controls the internal environment, is achieved by information flow connecting the components. The sensing of the external environment provides the stimuli for the action of the components.

Objective—A system has a purpose or objective. It is generally self-initiated, for a system achieves its goals by influencing the external environment or by modifying its relationship to the external environment.

The boundaries of a system are somewhat arbitrary. The lower limit of what can be classified as a system is set by the idea of a desired purpose or goal. Many components or procedures perform a specific function to perfection but in themselves achieve no purpose. The upper limit, or the number of functions that must be assembled before they may be thought of as a system, is troublesome. No matter how large the system, there will be some direct influence on the external environment, although it may be slight. The term "system concept," popularly applied as an approach to problem solving, implies an examination of all factors related to the problem. The boundaries of a system or problem could be expanded indefinitely with this logic. Of course, there must be some practical limit.

The most general implication—and perhaps the real importance—of the system concept is that of a series of interconnected elements, where changes in the external environment cause these elements to react in a cooperative manner to maintain system objectives. The fact that the reaction to any environmental change will follow a series of set rules allows the system behavior to be predicted. Systems may therefore be designed to achieve specific and useful purposes.

This chapter will briefly examine some of the various system elements, the methods of regulating their relationships, and the implications of these concepts for the design of management systems.

SYSTEM ELEMENTS

The general capabilities of the system will be composed of combinations of three basic elements—input, conversion, and output. The fundamental relationship of these elements is shown in Figure 5.1.

Figure 5.1. Elementary system model

Input—Data concerning the external and internal environment must be secured, transmitted, and classified. Events must be recorded in a form usable by the computer.

Conversion—The raw data must be converted into a form meaningful to the system purpose. This may involve any number of data-manipulation and logic operations. The conversion will follow some prescribable rules consistent with the objectives and purposes of the system.

Output—The results of the conversions must be transmitted to other system elements in a form they can recognize.

In an actual system these elements are combined in a variety of ways. They may be repeated, paralleled, and inter-related. Output from one set of elements may become input to another set.

CONVERSION METHODS

There are two general methods used to convert raw data to usable information—problem-solving and decision making. Problem-solving involves the prediction of results based upon the existing conditions of the variables and the known or as-sumed rules governing their interaction. Decision making in-volves the formulation of an appropriate response to the results of the problem-solving, such as the selection of the best alternative from a set of available alternatives. The prob-lem-solving must then precede the decision making, as illus-trated in Figure 5.2.

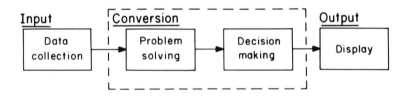

Figure 5.2. Conversion methods

Problem-solving may involve a variety of techniques to analyze the raw data and reduce them to meaningful form. There may be precise expressions of the relationships of variables. There may be forecasting methods which extra-polate history into the future. It may be as simple as com-paring actual conditions to a standard or to a plan.

58

Problem-solving must deal with both controlled and uncontrolled variables. Controlled variables have relationships which are ordered, and the response of the system to a change in a variable can be determined. This is not to imply that there are no statistical implications in the process response, only that they are known. Uncontrolled variables have cause and effect relationships beyond the control of the system, primarily those concerning the external environment, and therefore may only be reduced to probable responses to changes in the internal environment of the system.

The real management implication of problem-solving is typified by a "what if?" question. What if the unit price is increased? What if production output is increased 15 percent? What if the shipment is delayed another 10 days? In many cases the system is constantly asking itself this kind of question. For example, an inventory control system may be constantly predicting when stock will be depleted if there is no change in the demand pattern or order practice.

Decision methods are generally more complex than problem-solving methods. If the interaction of the variables is defined, the solution may be developed by one of the many mathematical optimization techniques. Decision making often involves intangibles and judgments which are too complex for specific definition, but it always implies a set of criteria by which the results of problem-solving may be evaluated.

CONTROL

The concept of decision making through some type of objective criteria introduces the principle of control. The use of feedback to control on operation is an important aspect of system theory. A simplified model of a control loop is shown in Figure 5.3. The three basic system elements are still pres-

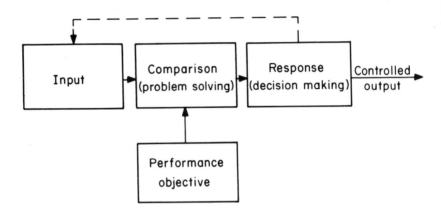

Figure 5.3. Control loop

ent. Again the input is the collection of data related to the environment of the process. The conversion process is now expanded to include the concept of the planned or desired performance of the process. The desired performance is compared to the actual performance, and any difference is reflected in the output. Based on this output, a response would be expected within the process which would change some aspect of the process and therefore modify the state of the system. This new level of activity would be sensed by the system through the input and again compared to the plan to assess the effectiveness of the response. In this way the system is constantly directed toward its objective.

The actual industrial or business organization will contain many control loops and loops within loops. Some of these will be fairly rigid and well defined. Others will be informal, and the potential responses will not be defined. Many decisions can be and should be accomplished by a computer, and the types of decisions that can be assigned to the computer are increasing. In business systems, however, many decisions are far too complex for specific definition and therefore must be assigned to people. The information system must support all required control mechanisms, both manual and programmable. Only if people have sufficient and proper information can they do a good job of handling complex situations requiring recognition, judgment, and discrimination.

In the man and machine system the control circuits may not be as recognizable as they are in mechanical-electrical systems; nevertheless, they do exist. It is sometimes difficult to isolate the role of the human decision elements of the system because the human being is capable of such extremely complex logic functions even in simple circumstances. For this reason it is vital to identify each of the steps in the control process. Allocation of duties must be made between man and machine. While it is frequently only practical that a man make the decision—for instance, when judgment is involved in a choice among alternatives—if the detail elements in the control process are identified, many problem-solving steps may be automated. However, as a class of situations becomes more frequent, it may be economically feasible to define the possible responses so that the system may automatically handle more of the decision making. Good systems design assigns to the man or the machine those elements which each does most efficiently. The design problem is frequently to provide an efficient interface between the man and the machine.

SUBSYSTEMS

All complex systems are made up of subsystems, and management information systems are no exception. Subsystems are separate parts of the total system which perform some specific useful purpose, but are not themselves of sufficient scope to be considered a system in the context of the total organization. A major benefit of subsystems is the organization of components in a way which will contain most of their interactions within the boundaries of a single subsystem. This provides easily definable design packages. It also localizes the problems that are found both in testing and maintaining the system, thereby greatly simplifying both.

Such classic departmental functions as quality control, cost accounting, inventory control. marketing, product planning, and engineering might be thought of as subsystems. Each of these departments has specific and somewhat independent responsibilities but, of course, must functionally interact with other departments to achieve the objectives of the organization. The subsystem concept, however, is not limited to such classic organizational functions. With an integrated information system there may be subsystems which are shared by several departments and therefore perform a service for the total organization. An example might be a subsystem which would develop forecasts to be used by several departmental subsystems.

The subsystem function, scope, and interrelationship with other subsystems may be defined in terms of information flow. An example is shown in Figure 5.4. In this example the product-planning subsystem establishes the basic requirements for the manufacturer of an item. These requirements are expressed in terms of such definite information as bills of materials, manufacturing operations, labor standards, and tooling. This information will be released to both the inventory control and the production control subsystems. These subsystems will process the information, compare required resources to available resources, establish the most feasible plan, allocate resources, and release the plan to the produc-

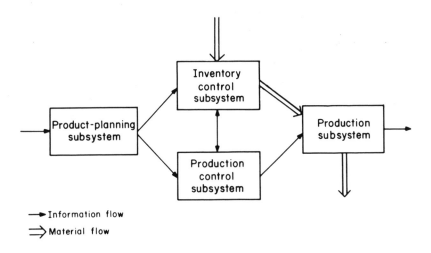

Figure 5.4. Information flow between subsystems

tion subsystem. The production subsystem will execute the plan.

When properly defined, subsystems will be independent of both material flow and physical constraints. It is therefore necessary only to define functional and information interfaces to have independent packages for design and development which will ultimately integrate properly with the total system. The concept of subsystems is therefore most useful in subdividing the system for either design or implementation.

THE TOTAL SYSTEM

Part of the system definition is the concept that the boundaries of the system enclose all components which directly interact. The system concept as applied to organizational behavior must then take into consideration all aspects

63

of the organization. The boundaries of the management system may enclose all functions of the organization.

The management process may be used to illustrate the concept of the total system. The management cycle has been divided into five steps, as shown in Figure 5.5.

Prediction—The management cycle starts with a forecast. This may concern predictions of basic parameters pertinent to the operation, such as sales, markets, and costs. It may also involve such things as statements of objectives, goals, policies, or technical changes.

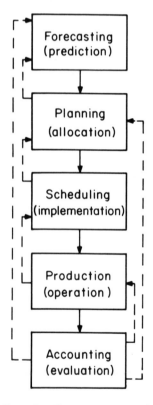

Figure 5.5. The management cycle

Allocation—The next step is a planning cycle. Alternate methods of deploying resources are evaluated. Interpretations and decisions may be made concerning the probabilistic aspects of the forecast.

Implementation—The implementation of the plan requires the assignment of specific resources to specific demands. Schedules may be established for manpower, material, facilities, and similar resources.

Operation—The plans and schedules must be executed. This production phase is designed to accomplish the basic organization objectives.

Evaluation—The actual accomplishments are compared with objectives, plans, and schedules, and evaluations are made of the differences.

Each of these management steps involves the processing of information. There must also be communication as the management responsibilities move from one step to the next. Forecasting must result in information that can be used for the planning of the operation. The information in the plan must become a vehicle for its implementation through scheduling. The schedule must be communicated to, and be understood by, those responsible for the actual production. The production process itself will generate much of the data necessary for management evaluation, a process classically known as accounting.

Some basic control features of an industrial organization are also shown in Figure 5.5. Each step in the management cycle involves one or more fundamental feedback loops. For example, the problems encountered during production may require reevaluation of schedules, and the deadlines imposed by the scheduling process may require revisions of plans. All other steps have similar control relationships.

From these relationships it is apparent that there must

65

be information compatibility between all steps in the management cycle. Each step must transmit information to the subsequent step, and therefore every step must interface with both its adjacent steps. Decisions in one step control the decisions that can be made in subsequent steps. There is a feedback type of control which involve all steps that operate by comparing data generated in one step with those developed in one or more prior steps. Conceptually, the entire management cycle therefore forms an integrated information system.

The general construction of the management system can be developed, as shown in Figure 5.6, by adding the system

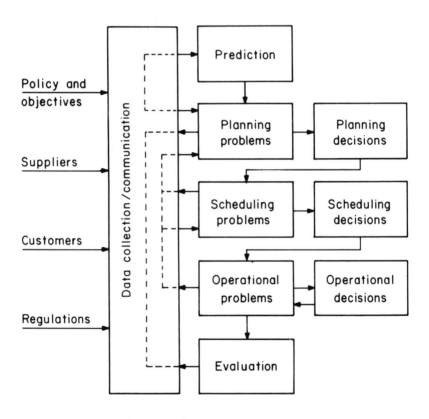

Figure 5.6. Elementary information flow

elements of data collection and problem-solving to the basic steps in the management cycle. Data are constantly collected. Such things as government regulations, customer desires, and supplier capabilities all provide facts about the external environment. Management policies and objectives define the alternatives available to the system. As the management cycle interacts, data are constantly exchanged.

Operational activity provides feedback for prediction, planning, and scheduling. The predictions generate problems which planning must solve. There must be decisions on planning alternatives before further action can be implemented by scheduling. Conflicts and problems arising during the operation of the plan must be solved by the scheduling subsystem; these decisions are immediately reflected in the operations. Complex and multiple control loops are operating to interrelate and to coordinate the action of the total system. The information flowchart, reflecting these information relationships, provides a general overview of the total management information system.

MODULAR DESIGN

The importance of this in-depth discussion of system characteristics is related to the necessity of dividing the information system into packages for both design and implementation. This subdivision of the total system is generally made necessary by the scope and size of the system, the need for concurrent design and development effort, and the evolutionary nature of management methods and systems. The selection of the proper modules is critical to the design effort in order to minimize total cost, expedite the development timetable, and maintain reasonable service as the system is developed.

67

The necessity of designing a system that can be readily modified and improved also adds importance to modular concepts. The management sciences elements of the system are part of a rapidly developing field. Continuing research and experience result in continuing improvements in many areas. The evolutionary nature of these techniques can cause rapid obsolescence in any system that is designed for a specific technique. If those aspects of the system can be isolated into easily replaceable modules, the economic impact of system improvement will be considerably lessened.

For example, consider an inventory system where stockroom issues are recorded, status records updated, predictions of future demands made, and a reorder level calculated. Each of the functions could be considered as a separate functional module. After the system was operational, experience and research might well show better ways to predict demands. If this occurred, it would be necessary only to replace or modify the prediction module, not the whole system. Design costs, testing problems, and interruption of normal operation would be minimized.

Those parts of the system which make such decisions as the calculation of the reorder level are subject to frequent policy changes (the availability of financing, government regulations, etc.). In these cases, it is generally necessary to implement the new policies quickly. Modular design makes this possible. This capability alone may well offset any cost that might be associated with module design.

When introducing a new system into an organization, it is frequently impossible to raise the operators and managers to the ultimate sophistication in one step. Each step in the implementation scheme should include only those changes which the organization can absorb at one time. Here again, the building block concept of modular design plays a key role. There are several reasons why, when installing the inventory system in the previous example, it might be decided to use existing forms and procedures to collect stockroom issue data, with a view to later providing remote data-collection capabilities. Here modular concepts would prevent complete redesign of the system when the data-collection capabilities were available. The programs and rules that collect and edit the data from the forms should be independent of the rest of the system. Even further, within this editing program separate modules for logical editing of each data element should be considered. Even if the actual program code could not be salvaged, the basic rules and logic could be used. The development of rules, logic, and policy is a major part of system design cost.

Proper definition of the system modules may allow standard parts of the system to be used in several places. This not only reduces development costs and time but also can improve reliability. For example, it might be necessary to check an activity message against a personnel file for validation and proper authorization of the sender. A standard program could be developed and used for all messages requiring this type of check. This reduces programming costs and provides a standard practice for all messages. Morever, the same program could be used if a new message were added to the system with assurance that it would work properly. This practice of standardizing subroutines (modules) is the basis for much of the software offered by computer manufacturers. The principles are equally valid for the development of systems designed for an individual organization.

The selection and designation of system functions as a module may occur at several levels. The subsystems may provide the major modules. There may be modules within modules. The depth at which separate functions should be formally identified as modules will depend on several factors in the scope and characteristics of the system. Some considerations are:

1. Those functions which may be subject to rapid obsolescence, either because of changes in policy or advances in the state of the art, should be confined in separate modules.

2. Where the implementation is to be done in phases, the modules to be included in each phase must perform a useful function themselves and must interface properly with modules to be included in subsequent implementation phases.

3. Any functional element which may be used several places within the system should be defined as a module so that it may be designed only once.

4. To be designated a module, a function must be capable of firm definition of such things as input-output in terms of data content, frequency, and response characteristics.

SUMMARY

The management information system integrates the activity of all departments within the organization. To accomplish this, it must involve all revelant interactions and relationships within the boundaries of the system. The system may be subdivided into functional parts called subsystems which perform specific missions within the system. Subsystems may be further subdivided into modules and into basic elements when functions may be more specifically defined. The basic elements are:

Input—The collection of data so that the status of the system's operational environment may be sensed.

Conversion—The processing of data so that alternatives may be formulated and operational decisions made.

Output—The transmission of decision and operation instructions to other elements within the system.

The system is constantly directed toward its objectives and goals through a series of feedback control loops. These control loops are constantly monitoring the operation and comparing the decision-making processes with predetermined standards (or objectives) to coordinate the actions of all system elements.

The understanding of system concepts allows the total system to be sectionalized into functional subsystems and modules. The principle of modular design is a major factor in the successful development of large systems, for it allows the efficient organization of the design effort and also facilitates the expansion and modification of the operational system, thereby retarding obsolescence.

6

Information Flow

INFORMATION CONTROLS the activity of any organization. Information is the basis for decision making. Decisions are translated into action programs, and instructions are transmitted to affected areas. Communication is the basis of coordination between various departments. The comparison of actions with goals forms the basis of control. In fact, most management functions involve information.

Information is also one of the major resources of the organization. The costs of developing and maintaining information are great. However, when costs are compared to potential value, the importance of the proper management of this resource becomes apparent. Accurate and comprehensive data promote better decisions and improved operations, benefits which may be an essential competitive advantage. Information is becoming recognized as a major asset of the organization, ranking with such resources as manpower, material, and facilities.

Information originates at many sources and must be transformed and transmitted to many action locations. In-

73

formation is generated by such external sources as government regulations, supplier policy, competition, industry practices, and, of course, customer requirements. The organization also internally generates great volumes of data, ranging from management policy and objectives, through research and development activities, to routine operating actions and decisions of the work force. The analysis of this information and the definition of the information flow network are major tasks in the design of any management system.

CHARACTERISTICS OF INFORMATION

The management cycle as discussed in Chapter 5 may be used as a very generalized model of the information needs of the organization. This type of information hierarchy is often shown in the form of a triangle, as illustrated in Figure 6.1. This triangle shows certain characteristics of information. The first characteristic is that everybody in the organization needs and uses information in the performance of his job. It also illustrates that considerably more detailed data are required during operations than during planning and policy cycles. For example, the production worker requires precise schedules, job instructions, and the like. The planning executive needs such summary data as production capabilities, backlogs, and costs.

This illustrates another characteristic. The same information will be used during several, if not all, steps in the management cycle. The difference in the several steps may be either the degree of abstraction or the method of presentation. For example, current production schedules must be constantly displayed at the operational level while the same data may only be needed on an exception basis during the scheduling process. The same schedules may be sum-

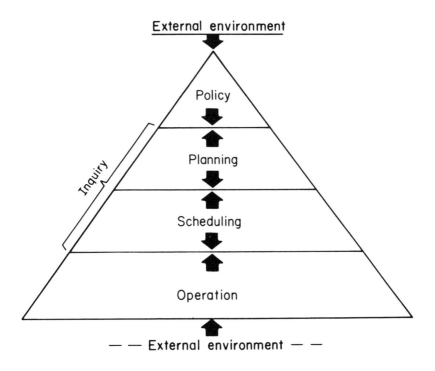

Figure 6.1. Information hierarchy

marized into overall backlog levels for the planning process. In this example the same underlying source data are therefore used at all levels but are displayed in less detail at successively higher levels.

Functional or departmental requirements have been added to the management cycle in Figure 6.2. Each step in the management cycle will involve such classic departmental functions as finance, production, and marketing (or perhaps, more precisely, each department will have its own cycle of planning, scheduling, etc.). The information needs of each department during any one step will be quite similar. For example, much of the information needed for market planning is basically the same as that needed for production

75

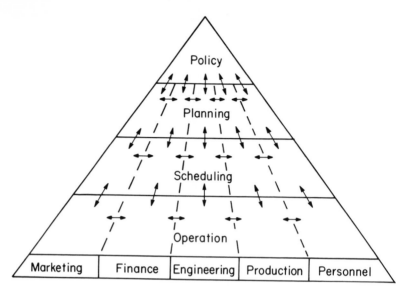

Figure 6.2. Functional information exchange

planning and personnel planning with, of course, much inter-
change of data between the planning functions. Therefore,
in addition to the vertical commonality of data, there is a horizontal commonality between departmental information needs.
A well-planned system will provide for all specialized departmental needs as a natural by-product of the basic information flow.

Information also has a time dimension. Its use and
value will change with time. Some data are transitory in
nature. They are used and then may be discarded. For example, a schedule priority is seldom of interest after the job
is complete. The value of other data will change significantly
with the timing of their availability. For example, the notice
of a delay in production schedule 10 hours in advance would
allow many more potential alternatives than if the same data
were known only one hour in advance. The value to the

organization is enhanced in this case by early notification. The converse may also be true; a detailed job schedule is of interest only to the production worker on the day he must take action.

The earlier discussion of the commonality of data exposed another time relationship. The same information may be used for different purposes at different points in time, and there may be different values associated with each use. The production schedule may be used to guide the production operation and later used to compare actual accomplishments to schedules for control purposes. The data may be essential to operations but merely desirable for control purposes. Some information may also change form with time, and there may be a change in value with the form. Production costs, for example, may be collected and audited in some detail but may be summarized at the end of an accounting period. The level of summarization, however, may affect both expense and value of the information. Detailed cost data may have value for analysis but would be expensive to provide. This type of situation touches on a problem in determining the information needs of an organization. Uses for information occur which are not routine and cannot be predicted much in advance of the need. These unknown needs are a difficult area, and inquiry capabilities will be covered in some detail in subsequent chapters.

THE DECISION PROCESS

Information flow in an organization is difficult to analyze and define. Where the information is transmitted without changing form, as might occur in a telephone system, the movement of data is not hard to follow. The problem is to determine the purpose of the transmission. However, where the information is converted from one form to another, as might occur in a computer system, the actual path is often obscure. Most information movement within the organization involves some type of conversion. When a message is transmitted from one person to another, facts are deleted or added, interpretations are made, limitations imposed. In other words, decisions are made. The flow of information is closely related to the decision process within the organization.

A decision in this sense involves a choice among various available alternatives. It is therefore not limited to management or policy decision but includes all the routine operating decisions that are made at all levels of the organization. The decision process itself is much the same whether it involves a machinist saving a few hours of set-up time or an executive spending several million dollars. A generalized model of the decision process, which uses the basic system elements of input, conversion, and output was discussed in Chapter 5. These elements are restated more in terms of information flow in Figure 6.3. Again there are the three basic steps:

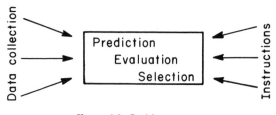

Figure 6.3. Decision process

Data Collection—All relevant available information is gathered, generally requiring the taping of several sources.

Decision Making—Alternatives are formulated and evaluated, and the most appropriate alternative is selected.

Instructions—Implementation instructions are communicated to the next step in the organizational process.

The next step in the process may be an action step (event), or it may be another decision. In fact, the total information flow within the organization might be viewed as a sequence or chain of decisions interconnected with actions and storage.

As an illustration of this relationship, consider the following example. Suppose trucks were dispatched daily from a warehouse. The trucks followed predetermined routes; assume that several sizes of trucks were available and were used depending on the actual load accumulated each day for the route. Assume also that a pool of drivers is available, but all drivers were not qualified to operate all sized trucks. The dispatch of the truck then requires the matching of load demand, truck capacity, and driver qualification. The decision process is illustrated in Figure 6.4.

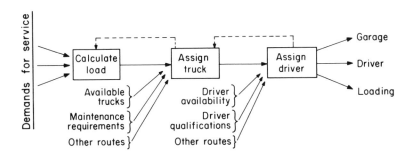

Figure 6.4. Dispatching a truck

The first step, or first decision, is to establish the load for the specific route. Demands for service are collected; sizes, weights, priorities, etc., are evaluated, and a consolidated load figure is developed. This is transmitted to the next step, where a specific truck is assigned to the route. This assignment must take into consideration, and therefore have information available on, such things as available trucks and

their capacities, the needs of other routes, maintainance schedules, and other factors. The output is a specific truck for a
specific route which must be assigned a driver. The driver
assignment will require a knowledge of available drivers,
their qualifications, and such things as the needs of other
routes, assignment rules, overtime, etc. When a decision has
been made on driver, truck, and load, instructions must be
sent to the driver and perhaps such other departments as
the garage (to prepare the truck) and the warehouse (to
prepare the cargo). In each case the organization must be
capable of notifying the preceding step, where a solution
cannot be made and other alternatives be evaluated.

Hence, there is a series of decisions, each involving information processing and communications. At each step information is collected and transformed to another set of information, which is transmitted to the next step, where more
information is collected, and so on. This process could be
physically accomplished in many ways. In a small operation
it could be one man who does all functions and gets his
information by looking out the window, so to speak. However, in a larger operation, where the volume required more
than one man, there would be a problem of the division of the
work load. The analysis of the specific information need for
each decision would be necessary before making this division.
The major new problem would be transferring facts and decisions from one man to the next. A computer program
could easily be developed for all or part of the process. Here
again, a prerequisite in either case would be an analysis
of each step for information input requirements and the output requirements for the next link in the process. New
management systems typically face this type of design problem. Several "black box" types of information-processing
steps are interspersed among several human processing steps.
The interfaces between the steps is information. This infor-

mation must be sufficient and must be transferred efficiently for the interface to be effective.

THE MAINSTREAM

If all the major decisions and actions in an organization were charted in some way, there would generally be a chain that weaves through the entire chart. Other decisions would feed into this chain, and decisions would branch from this chain. In fact, the sequence would probably touch on all the decisions in the organization and maintain a continuity through the entire chart. This sequence of decision is the primary channel where information naturally and necessarily moves to achieve the objectives of organization. This key information channel is sometimes called the mainstream.

The mainstream can be illustrated by returning to the example of dispatching the truck. In Figure 6.5 some logic elements of planning and operation have been added to the scheduling functions. Suppose that routes are established periodically to meet anticipated needs over some period of time. When routes have been established, there can be an evaluation of vehicle and driver pools required to support the routes. These planning decisions provide the basis for the scheduling decisions. When truck, driver, and load have been assigned to a route, there is a dispatch function by which all three are notified and released to actually operate the route. As the truck operates from point A to point B to point C, etc., data are generated which are used in subsequent planning and scheduling cycles. Actual loads, delays, priorities, and other factors help in planning future routes. Such things as mileage on the truck establish costs and maintenance schedules, etc. The driver's time is needed for payroll, availability, etc.

81

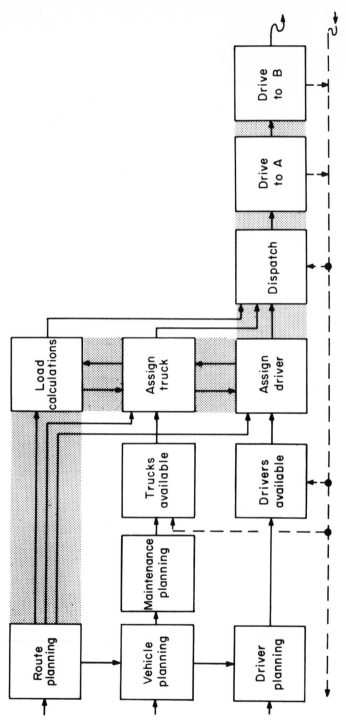

Figure 6.5. Trucking operation logic diagram

In this admittedly oversimplified example, there can be detected a key sequence of events and decisions, starting with the initial decision on routes and running through the daily assignment of specific trucks and drivers to routes and continuing through the actual dispatch and operation. Other information flows merely support the mainstream. It is interesting to note that after the truck is assigned, it becomes the focal point for all other actions. The driver and cargo tend to stay with the truck, and the events that occur to the truck generate most of the data required to support the scheduling and planning functions. If all the things that happen to the truck, such as starts, stops, delays, loading, unloading, were reported, it would also report all the things that happened to both the driver and cargo. The same thing cannot be said for either the driver or cargo. A system to "track" the movement of the truck would provide virtually all the information needed to manage the operation.

Most other organizations have similar key processes. In a manufacturing organization the movement of material from raw stock through processing into finished product would be the dominant process. The activities of people and the actions of the facilities would be secondary. The status of material flow could be determined by a tracking system which reported all the events that occurred to material and the operating decisions made about the material. For example, receipt of material, each operation accomplished, and each movement of material could be reported. Other events that occur, such as inspection, scrappage, and production delays, could also be reported. From these events the exact status of the production process can be determined. If sufficient data were reported about each event, there would be information available concerning such diverse things as inventories, machine loads, schedule status, quality control, performance measures, employee experience, and costs. A

83

system to track the material movement would generate almost all the data needed to manage the manufacturing organization.

The example of the trucking operation provides another insight into the flow of information in the organization. In Figure 6.5 the information flow between major logic steps was shown and no distinction was made between continuous and intermittent flows. During the scheduling process it was assumed, for example, that each time a truck was assigned to a route, there was a message sent to allow a driver to be assigned. In actuality there probably would be a schedule established assigning both trucks and drivers to routes for some period in the future. On a given day a message would be sent only if the truck type assigned were different from that in the schedule. Similarly, after the load calculation was made it would be necessary to notify the truck assignment element only if there was a change from the plan in the size of truck needed. There are other examples of exception reporting—that is, dispatch is interested in truck movement only in case of delays or other schedule interruption. In effect, what is occurring is that pools of information are being established about each resource—the trucks, the driver, and so forth. The pools contain such things as plans, inventories, capabilities, and current status. As decisions are made and events occur, they update the pools of information by adding to or changing the information they contain. Various actions or decision functions use the information from the pool at the time and to the extent needed. This type of information flow is charted in Figure 6.6.

The three major resources are shown—routes, vehicles, and drivers. The route-planning function uses policy plus experience data concerning each route to establish new routes. The vehicle-planning function uses the route information to establish changes in truck inventories or deployment. The

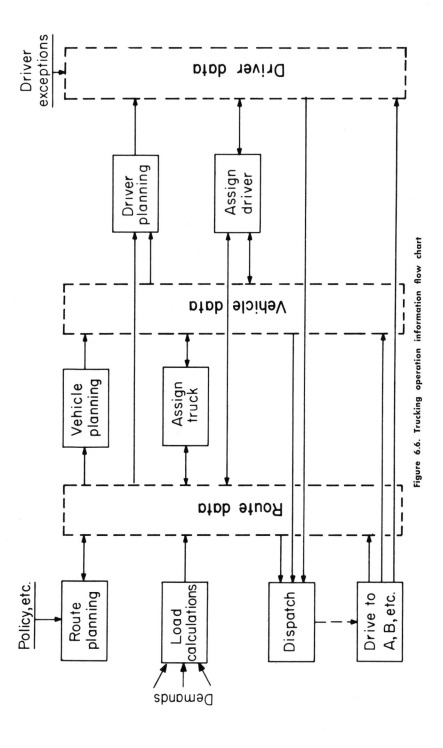

Figure 6.6. Trucking operation information flow chart

driver-planning function uses both route and vehicle data to recruit or train drivers and establish work schedules. The scheduling functions of truck and driver assignment are similarly using information from the pools and are also adding specific facts to the pool of knowledge, such as a specific truck on a specific day and specific route. Dispatch calls on all pools before a truck is released. The operation of the truck to its various destinations provides data to all pools. It will update the vehicle pool with status, mileage, repairs, costs, and the like. The movement of the truck will also update the driver pool with pay, experience, and other personnel data. In other words, the events that occur as the truck moves along its route will provide facts which can update several pools of information. These pools will contain the common information needed by such functions as the planning and scheduling elements and dispatch. Each function would depend on the common pool for the information needed to accomplish its mission.

These examples illustrate three major points in the design of management information systems, which have been mentioned before and will be covered in more detail in later chapters.

Data Bank—Most functional requirements are simply a specialized manipulation of general pools of information about major resources.

Event Reporting—A single report of key events along the mainstream will provide most of the data needed to update the major information pools.

Exception Reporting—It is possible to reduce the volume of information flow within an organization through exception reporting when such things as the plans, schedule, and status of a major resource are held in a common pool.

86

The identification and analysis of the information flow within the organization is one of the first steps in the design of any new management system. The existing information paths may be obscure due to physical and functional limitations which often make redundant communication and record-keeping necessary. However, an analysis of actual requirements of the total organization will reveal such things as the mainstream process and significant events within the process. Even where a system is to be implemented in phases, the total organization should be analyzed for information flow. Only with this knowledge can subsystem boundaries be defined and rational implementation packages be developed.

ANALYSIS METHODS

Perhaps we should discuss briefly the methods that are used to identify and analyze information flow. There are many specific techniques, such as flowcharts, decision tables, and data matrices, which can be used. However, before these tools can be employed, there is a fundamental question of the overall approach to the analysis task.

A frequent recommendation involves the study of the organization chart of job descriptions. This can be quite misleading. Information flow is not synonymous with classic organizational authority hierarchy as represented by an organization chart. Information is, of course, transmitted in the boss-subordinate relationship, but frequently the bulk of the actual communication is lateral flow between sections or departments at various intermediate supervisory levels. The informal relationships within the organization generally convey most of the key action information. Another recommendation is to review existing systems and procedures, either manual or computer, and to gather copies of forms and reports and to trace the movement of this paper. This review can be rewarding, as these procedures often constitute the only formal collection of organizational policy and philosophy. Existing systems, however, can also be misleading. They tend to be self-perpetuating even when the need has disappeared or the system has proved inadequate. On the other hand, informal systems frequently serve real needs, or they would be abandoned. These informal or semiformal systems may be difficult to discover and define but should not be ignored.

When looking at existing systems, either formal or informal, it is perhaps more important to study why they were established than how they operate. There are several questions that should be considered.

1. What are the management objectives of the procedure? What specific purpose and specific person is it designed to serve?

2. Is the purpose achieved and to what degree? Are the procedural requirements complied with? If not, what is the problem?

3. What is the relationship of this procedure to other procedures? Is there duplication of effort or data? Are there inconsistencies in results of various systems?

4. What problems are there, and what are the limitations of the procedure? What additional capabilities would be beneficial?

Of these questions, the last is perhaps the most important. This type of searching can reveal the real needs of the management. The present management methods may be due as much to systems limitations as to management intentions.

One very important set of facts can be gathered from a review of existing formal and informal systems. This is the language of the business—things such as the formal terms, the colloquialisms, the abbreviations, the codes. These words provide the core of the communications within the organization. It would be surprising if a study of this nature did not reveal many inconsistencies in any organization. The same term may have different meanings in different departments, several different terms may be used to describe the same things, or there may be subtle differences in the calculating statistics and ratios at various levels of management. These kinds of problems can be disastrous in any large information system. Perhaps one of the first steps in the analysis of information flow is the development of a standardized "dictionary" of terms.

Clearly, the initial step in the analysis of information flow is a fact-finding step. The fact-finding may include the study of existing procedures, interviews with operating and management personnel, or simply observation and research. However it is done, a major problem is where to start. There are perhaps only two places to start—at the top of the organization or at the bottom. The arguments for each method are something like this:

The analysis of information flow should start at the highest levels of management, where objectives and policy can be defined and where the important information needed by management to operate the organization can be determined. (Define the output reports, and this will automatically determine the input requirements.)

The analysis of information flow should start at the lowest level in the organization, where the operation can be defined and the information needed by successive levels of management to operate and control the organization can be determined. (Define the process and the feasible input and this will automatically determine the output needed to control the process.)

89

There is perhaps no one proper way to approach the problem. Much depends on the specific project and its scope. The top to bottom approach has a great deal of intuitive appeal. However, the second approach has many practical advantages, especially when design analysis is started. The study of the process will define the practical and meaningful points where information can be collected. The study can then proceed to the first level, where the information is significant in the direction and control of the process. From this point investigation can proceed laterally and vertically in successively larger control loops. This will define not only the information needs but also the decision points, man and machine interfaces, and, therefore, output requirements.

When the information network is deductively designed in the above manner, the inductive top to bottom approach affords an excellent means of validating the network. This is done by starting at the highest level of management involved and "walking" through the network to see whether it does meet the operating and control needs of management.

SUMMARY

Information flow may seem, when first considered, to be a nebulous concept. Information originates in many ways and many places. Part of the information will originate outside of the organization. Government regulations, supplier policies, competition practices, and customer requirements are examples of areas which will affect the information needs of an organization. Much of the data required for the organization will be internally generated from a variety of sources, including such diverse factors as management objectives and policy, in addition to routine factors such as operating decisions and actions of the organization.

Every organization has, to some degree, a body of formal

procedures and operating systems. In addition, there will invariably be a series of informal systems which probably handle much of the real operating data and decision making. The informal systems must take into consideration the tricky and often intangible contingencies of the actual environment at specific points in time. The variables involved will be numerous, and formal definition may be difficult. Nevertheless, the informal systems are an important part of the information flow of any organization.

Information has a multidimensional characteristic. Time is as important a consideration as location and content. Some information has a transient value; it is required for an operating decision and then is of no further interest. This information, however, must be available when the decision is to be made and must be available to all individuals who participate. Other information must be saved for subsequent action, review, or analysis. This retained information may be needed in several time frames. Facts about a future event may be needed only until the event has occurred. Other facts, such as the routine preparation of a profit and loss statement, may have recurring use. Much information has an irregular and unpredictable use and must be available on demand.

Information also has a universal characteristic. Any one fact may be of value to many departments within the organization. It may affect many different decisions. It will be summarized and analyzed in different ways for different purposes, but the source will be the same. Generally, these sources will be few. Within each organization there will be a key channel of information flow where continuity of organizational purpose is maintained and controlled. This key channel, or mainstream, is inevitably present within an organization even though it may be less apparent in organizations with less definable purposes.

These mainstream information channels will not correspond to the formal organization or to traditional management control functions, such as accounting, purchasing, engineering, production, inventory control, and similar departmental categories. The first step in developing a management information system is the identification and definition of the mainstreams of information flow. The basic data sources may then be systematically defined, classified, and organized. One of the primary objectives of the management information system is to make accurate and consistent information available to all departments and decision centers when they require it.

Only after these fundamental information processes and mainstream relationships have been defined can there be rational decisions concerning the design approach of the management information system. Specific areas may then properly be designated for initial concentration of system effort. Concurrent efforts can be initiated in several areas with a considerable degree of assurance that they will eventually interface into a total system. Similarly, the definition of data sources and the framework of the total system must be visualized before detailed design packages can be assigned to the many specialties which will ultimately become involved in the overall effort. Without the definitive synthesis of the mainstream information flow, it is inevitable that any fractionalized design efforts will result in incompatibility and frustrating disparities in functional interfaces. Conversely, a well-conceived master plan will allow management options in the selection of priority areas and will facilitate effective concurrent deployment of many resources toward a totally intergrated management system.

7

Activity Reporting

THERE IS A multitude of information available to the organization from both external and internal sources. The external sources are varied, depending a great deal on the nature of the organization. The internal sources, however, are more consistent and can be classified as (1) organization policy, which involves the procedures, rules, standards, and operating policies of the organization and (2) operating activity, which involves both the actions of people (events) and their day-to-day operating decisions.

Of the two types of source data, the operating activity is generally the more difficult to collect. There is a large volume of data that may originate at a variety of locations— all parts of the offices, warehouses, service areas, and production areas. These areas are frequently located in several widely separated cities. The activity data will also originate from a variety of people with different positions, skills, backgrounds, and so on.

This diverse group of people working at widely scatterd geographical locations must report many different types of

93

information, such as actions taken, decisions made, exceptions to plans, and related events, all of which must be recorded and converted to machine-usable language. It must then be validated for accuracy, and errors must be corrected and stored within the information system. The collection of data is generally one of the most difficult and expensive parts of the system design.

REPORTING EVENTS

In Chapter 6 it was shown that there are a limited number of key processes within any organization. The data-collection task is to report significant events that happen to these key processes. The proper selection of events to be reported is an important design task and can have great impact on the success of the system. The reporting points should, whenever possible, be physical events which can be recognized and identified as they occur. To provide current information and prevent loss of accuracy as time blurs memory, the reporting should generally be done as the events occur. The reporting requirements should follow the natural "flow" of the process. These natural breaks will remind the employee of the need to record data and provide a definition of the information content for both the reporting employee and the user of the data. This type of reporting aids in both compliance and accuracy.

It was also noted that many subsystems (functional responsibilities) require similar information about the same process. It is unnecessary and confusing to provide two sets of data about a single activity or process. If the selection of the reporting points is at a fundamental level, the data collected will support the needs of all subsystems. In many cases only exceptions need to be reported. This is possible when the exception condition is clearly definable and infrequent. If the exceptions are frequent and subject to interpretation, it may be best to report the actual operating environment and allow the computer to determine which are exceptions and how to classify them. This process can eliminate human bias and understanding problems. Here again, although a process may be subject to exception reporting for one function, the same process may require total activity reporting for another function. It is unnecessary to report both ways. The guidelines for good data collection might be summarized as follows:

1. Report the activity at the most fundamental level required for any subsystem.

2. Report each activity only once.

3. Report at natural breaks in the process.

4. Report basic facts; the computer may classify and cross-index.

5. The man taking the action should report the action as it occurs.

6. Reporting should be simple and convenient.

REPORTING DECISIONS

Some of the input to the system will concern events that are to occur sometime in the future. Basically these are operating decisions concerning the desired behavior of the system at some future time. Operating decisions are generally related to a specific circumstance and frequently limited to one-time application. The system design must allow these operating decisions to be reported at the time the decision is made.

95

Operating decisions can frequently be reported as exceptions to a standard operating plan. For example, a production plan is often created from a standard model. However, there certainly will be instances when the shop must deviate from the plan. In this case the shop should report the change in plan to the system. The alternate plan should then be evaluated by the system at least to the extent of an assurance that there will be no catastrophic consequence in some other shop or at some other time. All the records in the system should be updated and the system should inform any areas which require coordinated action.

METHODS AND EQUIPMENT

There are many ways to convert human language to machine language; in any one system a variety of combinations may be used. The classic method is to send handwritten documents to the computer. This is generally accomplished by routing documents to a keypunch department for conversion to punch cards for subsequent reading into the computer. There are several disadvantages to this method. Among them are the potential of clerical error, the cost, and the time spent in simply handling the documents. A significant improvement in the central conversion process has resulted from the development of optical character readers (OCR), which can "read" printed information and translate it into a computer language. These devices vary in capability from a simple machine with the ability to read special print fonts to very versatile equipment which can even read handwritten documents. All of these devices, however, still have the disadvantage of time, cost, and error potential because of the handling of documents at a central location.

The development which has perhaps done more than

anything else to make management systems practical is the remote data-collection terminal, which can be placed almost anywhere in the factory, warehouse, or office. These devices are activated by an employee and transmit information over wires to the computer. The advantages of this method include a reduction in clerical cost and error and the rapid availability of data. This method of data collection is becoming so important that there is an ever increasing number of devices on the market. At the present time the devices can rather arbitrarily be classified into three groups.

Card Readers—Fixed data are prerecorded on a card of some type by such methods as punched holes and magnetic encoding. An employee inserts the card containing fixed data into the device and then enters variable information, and a message containing both the fixed and variable data is transmitted to the computer. The variable information can be entered in several ways—turning dials, moving levers, or pushing buttons. The card readers generally have a certain amount of ability to check for errors before sending the message.

Keyboards—Several kinds of devices have typewriter-type keyboards. Frequently they appear as a regular typewriter and are used for both input and output—for example, a question is typed on the keyboard, and the answer is printed on the paper.

Direct Reading—Several kinds of devices might be classified as direct reading devices. For example, a transmitter could be connected to a machine tool to record when the machine was turned on and off. The computer could use these data for calculating machine utilization. Similarly, a device might be attached to a cash register to record transactions for subsequent processing by the computer. The advantage of these devices is they do not require additional conscious effort on the part of the operator.

97

Outputs from other systems can become input to an information system. There are many mechanized systems which probably cannot be considered part of the management information system but which do utilize much numerical information in the process of achieving their purpose. Selected parts of this numerical information may be extracted and utilized in the management system. Some examples may illustrate the principles.

Numerical Controlled Machines—Metalworking companies have used numerical control (NC) machines for some time. These machines use a punched tape, possibly prepared by a computer, to provide logic control of the metal-cutting operation. In a more advanced form called direct digital control (DDC), he machine tool is online with a central computer which contains the logic instructions for the operation and will control several machines. At the same time the central computer can compile a record of the machines it controls. Data on production counts, costs, delays, and related information are gained by direct interface with the production process.

Automated Warehouses—Many advances are being made in mechanizing warehouses. Upon command, machines can automatically locate and retrieve any product from the warehouse. With proper interfaces to a central computer the devices can automatically record receipts, issues, inventory balances, and similar data, all of which are of interest to the management information system.

Medical Examinations and Tests—Many medical examinations and laboratory tests can now be performed by various types of automated equipment. When data resulting from these tests are fed into a controlling computer, it not only can aid in diagnosis but can also provide an information system with valuable data for such diverse purposes as billing and patient histories.

There are many other examples where "islands of automation" are interfaced with the management information system. Automated process industries, such as oil refineries and chemical plants, provide several examples; automated test equipment and test cells provide other examples. The advantages are numerous—reduced data-collection costs, direct control, and rapid feedback, to name a few. There are, of course, problems in both complexity and proper design approach.

In addition to the machine-to-machine communications, there are methods where a combination of machine language and human language may improve the efficiency of the input processing. Utility billings are an example. The statement is both printed and punched into the same card. When customer returns the payment with the prepunched card, the card becomes a machine-language input to the system. Another example is prepunched cards used in remote-transaction recorders, where the card is used to identify the process and is both printed and punched. The special characters preprinted on checks are yet another example of turnaround documents. These magnetic ink characters can be read by special devices and converted into machine language for computer processing, a development that has greatly aided the banking industry but is generally limited to it.

PROCESSING METHODS

Once source data are available to the computer, there are basically two ways that they may be processed. Batch processing involves holding the data until a quantity, or "batch," of similar information is available. The batch is then read into the computer, where it is processed. Online processing presents the data to the computer as data become available, and each message is processed as it is received. Figure 7.1 illustrates these two methods.

The batch processing is frequently used when the com-

99

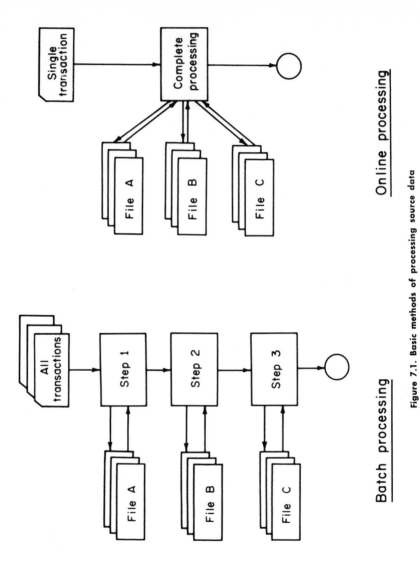

Figure 7.1. Basic methods of processing source data

puter storage is limited or when response or file currency is not critical. To illustrate, assume a message reporting an issue from stock. Batch processing would proceed somewhat as follows:

1. Sort all input by type message.
2. Edit for correct format.
3. Sort to sequence by part number.
4. Match to inventory file.
5. Update inventory file.
6. Print list of errors.

The online processing is essential where rapid response is required; however, online processing does not necessarily imply rapid response. In this method each message is processed completely before any work is done on the second message. Using the inventory issue message as an illustration, the processing would proceed somewhat as follows:

1. Identify the message.
2. Obtain required file data.
3. Edit and validate complete message.
4. Print any required error notices.
5. Update inventory files.
6. Select next message.

ACCURACY CONTROL

Formal management control and decision-making capabilities can be no better than the information which is used as a foundation for these capabilities. Errors in basic source data can result in unwise decisions and inefficient operations. Errors can create a lack of confidence in the system and ultimately are manifested in the organization missing potential opportunities for improved management. Even minor mistakes can alienate customers, suppliers, and employees. Controlling the accuracy of source data must be a critical design consideration. However, accuracy can never be absolute. There must therefore be a careful evaluation of economically acceptable error rates that, at the same time, provide protection against serious mistakes. The system itself should provide more or less automatic controls to ensure that design assumptions are achieved in the actual operation of the system. The problem providing accurate input may be divided into three phases—prevention of errors, detection of errors, and correction of errors.

Prevention

The prevention of errors starts with a sound basic design of the collection system. Only the minimum essential data about an occurrence should be reported. There is little benefit in telling the system something it already knows. The person who accomplishes an action should generally report the action to the system. This minimizes the likelihood of errors in interpretation, intent, and transcription. Simplicity in message content and convenience in recording also assist in accurate input.

As noted above, it is generally preferable for the individual accomplishing the activity to report the event. He knows precisely what occurred and is not as subject as a second person to interpretation or transcription errors. The man who takes the action is also in a position to report immediately after the action has occurred, thereby providing current information to the system. In an effort to increase accuracy, specialized clerks are sometimes used to report activity. This is frequently self-defeating. If the system is simple, the clerk is subject to about as many random errors as the employee who took the action; moreover, the clerk is subject to interpretation errors. There are the other obvious disadvantages of duplicate effort and timing problems. Most errors are errors of omission—the complete failure to make any report—a problem over which the clerk has no control. If the system design is simple and follows real-life rules, the employee who is involved in the activity has greater resources and generally greater motivation to provide accurate information.

When using remote data-collection devices, there are several design objectives in composing the message. The foremost is to minimize the selections and actions that the operator must make. Experience seems to indicate that accuracy deteriorates exponentially as the number of variables per message increases. There also seems to be a significant difference in the accuracy resulting from the different methods of entering the data. Push buttons appear to be better than either dials or levers in most circumstances. Prepunched cards and preprinted forms that identify fixed data can also reduce operator problems.

Detection

All types of errors should be detected at the earliest possible time. The farther an error penetrates the system, the more difficult it is to correct. The detection must include errors of both omission and commission. The errors of commission are generally format or validity problems and can be detected by such normal computer editing as format checks and range checks.

In a format check the message may be checked for the proper number of characters and the proper combination of alphanumeric characters. Spacing and punctuation can also be checked. If the value of the characters is limited in parts of the message, a range check can be made for conformity with these limitations. For example, if only numbers 1 through 5 were legitimate codes, the number 6 could be rejected.

Errors of omission, when there was a failure to send any message, are far more difficult to detect. Recognition depends on the logic of the system. A lot of ingenuity applied to a specific system is required to design the detection rules. The following examples will illustrate some possible types of rules:

Preceding Event—A truck cannot arrive at its destination unless it has departed from its origination point.

Impossible Situation—Two trucks cannot simultaneously park at a single loading ramp.

Correction

All errors should be detected as soon as possible. The longer the time from the occurrence of the action, the more difficult it is to determine who made the mistake, exactly what the mistake was, and what the correct data should be. If any processing is done with the data before an error is detected, it is necessary not only to find the correct data but also to undo the erroneous processing.

Most data-collection devices will immediately reject messages when errors are detected by the computer. The depth of immediate editing depends on computer configuration and system design, and the simple notification of a reject may be insufficient to allow a person to recognize his mistake.

A more effective method of processing data is the online, or so-called real-time, system, because it provides a complete and immediate edit before the file update is performed and any errors are immediately transmitted back to the person making the message. Immediate corrective action may be taken while the source information is still available. These systems, however, require rather elaborate computers and two-way terminal capabilities. Therefore, they have been considered quite expensive in the past; recent developments, however, have made consideration of this type of system quite practical. Recognition of the value of accurate and timely data and elimination of retroactive error-correction cost have made real-time data collection attractive even in smaller information systems.

Where it is impossible to provide an immediate response to an error, a decision must be made as to the disposition of an incorrect message. There may be cases where the computer may deduce the correct data from the message content and other related data. The message may then be rejected in total or in part. In any case, where all or part of the message is rejected, some person must be notified of the rejection. Whenever a message is rejected, care must be taken to assure that the remainder of the message does not cause another error in subsequent processing. Two error notices concerning the same event can be confusing in the effort to unscramble the erroneous processing.

A printed notice will generally signal the detection of an error. Whenever practical, the notice should be directed to the person who originated the message, on the assumption that he is best prepared to know the correct information. However, in some cases it may be more efficient to send error notices to a central records group if the editing of the input is infrequent and the original data are no longer

105

available to the originator. In some cases, however, this practice may have a detrimental psychological effect in that the originator "got by" with the mistake.

The correction of errors should generally be made as convenient as possible. Error notices should be in a readable form and use terms meaningful to the originator. To facilitate correction, the notice itself should be reenterable—that is, the originator should be able to correct the errors in the message and return the amended notice to the computer system. Another aid is to provide the originator with any supplementary information available in the system that may ease the investigation and correction of the error.

Follow-up and Control

Whatever technique is used to detect and correct errors, some form of follow-up and control must be established to ensure that errors are minimized and properly corrected when they do occur. There are several schemes to accomplish this. One type requires a positive action on every error detected. If corrective action has not occurred within a prescribed time, a second notice is prepared. Or a follow-up may be sent to the supervisor of the employee. This is not always successful because a supervisor cannot cope with the detail and because it is costly in terms of redundant output. Whatever method is used, it seems essential to assign errors to departments and to prepare summary reports at all responsible levels of management. Each level of management must accept the responsibility for the accuracy of that portion of the system that is under its jurisdiction.

THE SHOP ORDER SYSTEM

It is apparent that there are many data-collection methods available, and the appropriate methods will depend upon the needs of the system. A somewhat standard method has been adopted by many manufacturing industries to meet their special needs. This procedure is frequently called the shop order system. The shop order example was selected not so much as a model to be used in other areas but as an example to illustrate how some of the principles of reporting simplification, integration, and standardization may be applied. These principles provide powerful tools which may be applied in other areas, especially when reporting from remote locations is required.

General Flow

The shop order system is used to control paper work and to report production status to a computer system. The system includes computer-printed routing documents, activity reporting to the computer from remote locations, and status monitoring and control by the computer.

As the name of the system implies, the key document is the shop order, an example of which is shown in Figure 7.2. The shop order is basically an identification, routing, and work-sequencing document. It contains the information necessary to identify the product, such as the part number and part description. It also contains a list of the operations (routing steps) to be performed. The general procedural flow of the shop order system is shown in Figure 7.3. The first step is the release of a job by an induction notice to the system. The system matches the product to be produced with a production planning file to determine the routing and manufacturing requirements. One of the documents produced

107

Part number	Lot number	Quantity	Control number
47092-356-A	AK-1624	015	19632

Part description
BRACKET FRONT-WHEEL ASSEMBLY

Line	Work center	Work description
01	296	CUT TO LENGTH
02	283	DRILL HOLES (2)
03	296	FORM
04	287	PAINT
05	270	INSPECT

4709 - 356-A	BRACKET	19632
Part number	Part description	Control number

Trigger card

Figure 7.2. Shop order and trigger card

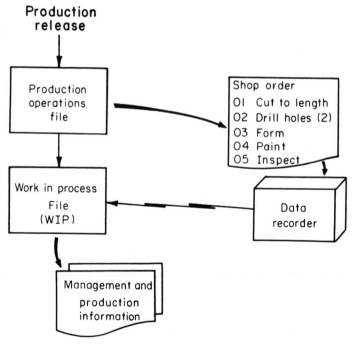

Production
release

Production operations file

Shop order
01 Cut to length
02 Drill holes (2)
03 Form
04 Paint
05 Inspect

Work in process File (WIP)

Data recorder

Management and production information

Figure 7.3. Shop order flow

is the shop order. Other documents might include production schedules, machine loads, and similar production control information.

Activity Reporting

When the shop order is printed, identical data are placed in the computer suspense file, frequently called the work-in-process file (WIP). A key element of data in the suspense file is the control number (CN). This computer-assigned number is printed on the shop order and also becomes the record identifier in the suspense file. In the illustration in Figure 7.2 it is the number 19632 in the upper right-hand corner. The control number is a document serial number which identifies a specific unit or batch. Any reporting to the computer will use the control number to identify the job being reported. A prepunched card is also produced for each shop order. It contains essentially the same identification data as the shop order and is called a control card, a follower card, or a trigger card, as shown in Figure 7.2. This card is prepunched with the control number of the shop order and is used in data-recording devices to send messages to the computer concerning the shop order. The data recorder can "read" the control number punched in the trigger card after it is inserted in the device. Compared to any other identification, such as part number, the control number is a simple standardized number; thus, this procedure minimizes both transmission time and potential error. (The part number and account code are cross-referenced to the control number whenever the system needs such information.)

When production status is being reported, information which will change with each message will be required. Data recorders have buttons, dials, or levers which can be used to transmit this variable information. One kind of variable information is the type of message. A transaction code such as the following is used for this purpose.

Code 1—Completion of an operation.

Code 2—Quality reject.

Code 3—Rescheduling of an operation.

Code 4—Part scrapped.

Other variable information, such as date and time, may be automatically supplied by the data recorder.

For much of the production status reporting, it is also necessary to identify the operation involved. Each operation on the shop order is given a sequence number, called a line number. Because the computer suspense file (WIP) contains the same data as the shop order, it is necessary to report only the line number to identify an operation to the computer. For example, in Figure 7.2 the line number 2 would represent the operation "drill holes" to the computer for shop order 19632. This line number would be entered in the variable data section of the data-recording device when activity about that operation is reported.

The message content, then, consists of four sections:

1. Process Identification—The prepunched control number in the trigger card.

2. Message Identification—A transaction code identifying the nature of the activity entered in the variable section of the data records.

3. Operation Identification—A line number identifying the manufacturing task or step involved, entered in the variable section of the data recorder.

4. Time and Date—Time and date are automatically supplied by the data recorder. The man reporting action

against the shop order therefore follows the rather simple procedure of inserting the trigger card and then entering the line number and the transaction code.

Supplementing the message identity, there may be other variable information, such as the number of parts scrapped, which could be entered in the variable section of the data recorder. From the combination of this information, any pertinent event that occurs to the part during the manufacturing process can be reported to the system.

When the message is received by the computer, it is matched to its WIP record. After a comprehensive editing each message results in a corresponding change to WIP record. This constantly updated WIP record, which represents all events that have occurred in the manufacturing process, can be used to derive a comprehensive status report of the manufacturing process and to transmit this status to operating management in whatever form is required.

Labor Reporting

The system can also be used to record labor costs (labor distribution) against each shop order. In this program each employee is issued a card with his employee identification number that can be read by the data recorder. The employee then reports every time he stops working on an operation, using the shop order trigger card and his employee identity card. The computer than elapses time from one job stop to the next to establish the time spent on each job.

The computer will contain a record of each employee, relating his employee number to such data as his name, work location, and current shift assignment. If the employee starts work on time, he makes no report until he completes his first job. Assume that the employee starts to work at 8:00 and completes his first job—which is line 01, "cut to length"—at 10:00. He would report at 10:00, using his identity card and the shop order trigger card, entering variable data showing the completion of line 01. The computer would subtract the 10:00 stop from the 8:00 start and conclude that he spent two hours on operation 01. The start of his next activity would be assumed to be the end of job 01, or 10:00. This next activity could be an indirect activity, such as "go to medical," in which case a card similar to the trigger card would be provided for the medical code. These examples are shown below:

EMPLOYEE	CN	LINE	TIME	ACTIVITY DESCRIPTION	M/HRS.
7016	19632	01	10:00	Cut to length	2:00
7016	99999	00	11:15	Medical	1:15
7016	19632	02	11:45	Form	0:30
	Date recorder			Suspense file	Calculation

In this way the system records how each employee spends his day, in addition to exact production status.

Through a series of relatively simple messages from the production floor, the system is able to obtain a variety of information from one simple document. Because of the availability of this information, including man-hour distribution and progress status, the system is able to produce the reports and documents required to plan, schedule, and monitor the work flow, much of which can be on an exception basis. The system can also provide performance analysis in such critical areas as product cost, machine utilization, work-load planning, and manpower utilization. This type of activity reporting in an integrated information system can quickly identify problems and can therefore lead to more timely decisions by well-coordinated management teams.

SUMMARY

There have been many recent improvements in the methods and machines used to collect the basic information essential to any management information system. Data collection, however, still remains an expensive and troublesome aspect of the system. Accuracy is a continuous problem and must be a consideration during the entire design process. Because data collection is usually a man and machine interface, these considerations must come from both the behavioral and communication-computer sciences.

8

Data Organization and Storage

THE MANAGEMENT SYSTEM must store the vast amounts of information that it receives, in addition to being able to locate and retrive any part of this information on demand. Some of the demands will be well defined, such as periodic payroll or accounting needs; however, other demands for information may occur more or less at random, such as an inquiry to trace a missing shipment or a request for an order delivery date. Some demands may not even be apparent at the time of system design. These unknown needs may be single occurrences, such as a special study, or they may be routine information needs that are discovered after the system is operating. The management system must service all of these needs of the organization.

The computer's storage capabilities can be a significant part of the hardware cost of the system. Similarly, the classification and retrieval of information can be a significant part of the processing cost of the system. Conversely, the sufficiency and availability of basic information will directly affect the degree to which the system can satisfy the needs of the organization. The tradeoffs required in this area cause the design of the basic data-storage structure to be an important aspect of the system design.

DATA ELEMENTS

The language of the real world is too complex to be used by the computer. Although the use of natural language by computers has been the subject of considerable research in recent years, the real-world language must still be structured and disciplined for use in the information system. This can be accomplished by dividing information into data elements, or fields, as they are sometimes called.

The data element is the lowest identifiable division of information within the information system. The data element is treated as a discrete entity,—that is, it is stored, addressed, and treated as a complete item in all ways. This division can be quite arbitrary, depending only on the use to be made of the data. Suppose that there were a file of customers in which each customer was identified only by his name and address. If this data were for reference only, the complete identification could be a data element. However, suppose that someone wanted to print mailing labels. It would then be necessary to divide this data into three data elements: (1) customer name, (2) street address, and (3) city and state. Further, suppose that for some reason it was desirable to organize lists of customers by state and city. It would then be necessary to separate city and state, thereby creating four data elements: (1) customer name, (2) street address, (3) city, and (4) state. The data element is therefore an abstract division of information. The information within the boundaries of the data element will vary with the nature of the data but can be rather free form. It is therefore difficult, and some-

116

times impossible, to subdivide a data element once it is established in an operating system.

The rigorous definition of data elements is essential to the success of the system. Each must have a clear and distinct meaning. Each should also have a meaningful title or label. This title must be consistently used whenever the information appears. A comprehensive dictionary or library of data elements is indispensable in the design and use of the system. This point cannot be overemphasized. The most technically proficient system will be useless unless the language is consistent and understandable to all users.

TYPES OF DATA ELEMENTS

The various sources of information available to the organization will provide several different types of data elements. For convenience they may be classified as static elements, dynamic elements, and historic elements. The static elements consist of policy, planning, and procedural information. The dynamic elements consist of status or "tracking" information that changes as activity occurs. The historic elements consist of a mixture of static and dynamic elements about past events. The storage problems and design requirements are slightly different for each type of data element.

Static Elements

Static elements are generally basic facts about a process or person which are changed only by fundamental changes in the process itself. As such, they represent planning, policy, an operations file, or an employee data file. This type of data is generally supplied by planners, analysts, and similar individuals. It is generated by the correlation of several

117

sources, research, or creative thinking. This presents the major problem—file development and maintenance.

To develop the file data, it is necessary for the information to be organized, converted to standard terms, and written in a standard manner. The design objective is conversion of the data to a standard form as early in the generation process as possible. To illustrate, assume a production-planning file which contains manufacturing operations, bills of materials, standard costs, and similar information for every product. The data for this file start with the engineering design. At some point in the engineering process, information can be recorded on a standard form to start building the file. Information could be added by production engineering, methods engineering, and other groups that contribute to the total information on the product.

Provisions must be made to revise the files as fundamental changes in the product or process occur. File maintenance can become an expensive aspect because of the ever-increasing cost of engineers' and planners' time and the necessity of providing rapid changes to the file. If a change in policy or process affects several files, provisions should be made to update all files simultaneously by a single input. In general, the objectives of file maintenance methods are human convenience and efficiency, with little regard for computer efficiency.

Dynamic Elements

Dynamic elements contain facts about the status and perhaps the immediate plans of a given environment. They are updated by reporting pertinent activities within the organization and are therefore subject to frequent and random changes as operational events occur. An example would be a work-in-process file or an inventory file. The demands on these files are considerable. Therefore, the structure of these files must have sufficient logic and contain sufficient data from the viewpoint of the process to allow rigid validation of incoming activity reports. A specific activity report may be used to update several categories of information. To illustrate, assume an activity report which says, "Lot 69 was produced by J. Smith on lathe 22." This event could have impact on such information elements as machine utilization for lathe 22, labor distribution for J. Smith, and job status for lot 69. It might be necessary to check all three sources— machine status, employee status, and job status—before the activity report can be completely validated and all files updated.

Historic Elements

Historic elements include past events that are no longer pertinent to the current operation. They must be retained, however, for planning, evaluation, and accounting purposes. The problems in this area depend greatly on the type of organization, the type of system, and the computer configuration. One general problem is establishing interrelationship and cross-indexing between different data elements so that any new analysis requirements can be met from historic data. History generally involves a great volume of data and therefore storage costs can become critical. However, this is somewhat offset by the fact that generally the need for rapid access (retrieval) is not great, as it is with other types of information.

SELECTION OF DATA

It is generally recognized that the needs of the organization will change. Problems change, tighter controls are required, experience with information generates demands for more sophisticated analysis. Many of these needs cannot be anticipated at the time the system is designed. One of the measures of the success of a management system is its flexibility in adapting to new requirements of the organization.

A key question when considering flexibility of storage is the depth at which information elements should be retained. Production count can illustrate this point. Information could be stored for each piece or lot that was produced, it could be summarized daily by product, it could be summarized weekly by product group, or so on. It is apparent that the greater the summarization, the less the storage cost. However, succeeding levels of summarization reduce the analysis potential of the data. For example, weekly summaries cannot be directly converted into monthly summaries and vice versa; similarly, if the production count was summarized by day, it would never be possible to conduct an analysis of productivity by shift. In general, if information is stored at the event level, the system can respond to most practical demands for new and special output information.

A closely related question is the amount of detail that should be recorded about each activity. Even though the information is recorded at the event level—namely, production by piece part—there remains the question of how many facts should be recorded about each event. There might be supporting facts, such as lot number, part number, date, and time, all of which could be recorded as the count was recorded. These subordinate facts may not be required for immediate use, but they do provide a strong base for expansion and response to special requirements.

CODING AND CLASSIFICATION

Natural language can also be structured by various coding and classification schemes. These codes are not necessarily those used for security or efficient data transmission but, rather, are methods used in commercial practice to systematize the recording of information. These codes are familiar to everyone—the part numbers that are used for almost all manufactured parts, the ZIP code numbers used by the post office, and the social security numbers.

There are many types of codes. The simplest is a sequential code, wherein a list of items is numbered sequentially, starting with one. Another common method is block coding. In this method both the value and the position of the number have significance. Suppose that in a customer file it were necessary to associate statistical data, such as the type and size of firm, with each of the customers. The following sequential codes could be established:

TYPE OF FIRM		NUMBER OF EMPLOYEES	
Code	Description	Code	Description
01	Manufacturing	01	0—100
02	Finance	02	100—500
03	Utility	03	500—1000
04	Sales	04	over 1000

A four-digit block code could then be used to identify customer type and size. The first two digits would be type, and the last two would be size. The code 0201 would then represent a finance firm with fewer than 100 employees.

A combination of sequential and block coding may be used to indicate the hierarchical position of a data element. The ZIP code is an example: The first digits identify the city, and the last digits identify the zone within the city. Another example is the manufacturing assembly diagram, frequently called a "GOZINTO" (goes-in-to) file. In this file the item's position in an assembly hierarchy is shown through identification numbers. Consider products which break down into assemblies, subassemblies, and piece parts. All assemblies could be assigned a sequentially developed identity code. Within each assembly all subassemblies could be sequentially numbered. Similarly, all piece parts within a subassembly could be given a sequential number. Each number would then have a unique meaning only when associated with the number of the higher-order assembly. A code could be established with three blocks, as shown in Figure 8.1. Code 62 00 00 would be the end assembly itself. Code 62 02 00 would be subassembly number 2 within that assembly. Finally, the piece part code of 62 02 01 would uniquely identify both the part and its position in the assembly hierarchy. This type of hierarchical problem is encountered in the data structure of many aspects of organizational information.

The importance of coding systems should not be minimized. With or without computers they frequently represent the most formalized aspects of an organization's operating procedure and as such have a significant impact on the efficiency and manageability of the operation. The codes should be designed with sufficient flexibility and scope so they can cover the total operation, including exceptions, and can be expanded into additional areas if this should be required. The code structures should be free from ambiguities and should be logical, convenient, and meaningful for all who must use them.

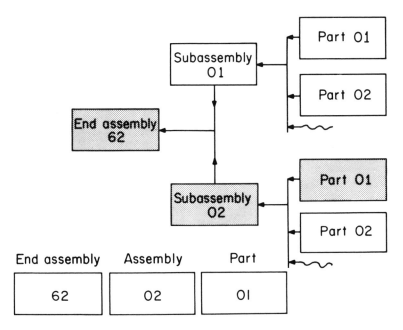

Figure 8.1. "GOZINTO" type of hierarchy code

ORGANIZATION AND INDEXING

Problems of data management involve a series of both technical and practical considerations. It does seem important to look at some of the largely technical considerations of file organization and indexing. All data elements in the information system must be organized in a fashion that allows logical and orderly access to each data element. The basic approach is to group related data into records. A series of records constitutes a file. In computer jargon these terms have the same meaning as they do for any office filing system. The only problem in either system arises when it is necessary to use a record or series of records that are in the file. For this purpose each record must have an index, or key, which

123

may be the subject or title of the record. In a file of employees the key could be the employee number or social security number.

If someone wanted to obtain all the information about employee 69201, he would have to have access only to record 69201. This may be done in two ways. He could start at the front of the file and examine all records until 69201 was found; this is a file scan or sequential access. If only one employee record was of interest, this method would be inefficient and time-consuming. Therefore, most file systems, both manual and computer, are designed so that the record of interest may be found without reference to all other records in the file; this is random, or direct, access.

The problem in the management system is further compounded because what is generally needed is not a complete record but, rather, a data element or series of data elements in one or more records. We may, for example, be interested only in the names of electricians who are less than 35 years old. Two of the general solutions to the problems of direct access to specific data elements are (1) independent index and (2) linkage, or chain. To solve the problem of selecting the names of electricians from the employee file, we could establish a duplicate subsidiary file which was organized (indexed) by craft. It would be a simple matter to enter the subsidiary file where the craft "electricians" started and retrieve all the names filed under that category. However, in the interests of storage economy, the subsidiary file might contain only the employee number. This file would then "point" to the proper record in the master file, where the names could be found. Hence, we would link, or chain, from one file to the next by use of a "pointer." The problem of the age of the electricians could be solved in a similar way.

An example of the need for a complex index between files and records occurs in production and inventory control, generally called a bill of material program. In the production assembly file (GOZINTO) shown in Figure 8.1, let us assume that an inventory is maintained of all subassemblies and piece parts and that piece parts may be used in several subassemblies. Further, suppose that we wish to use an inventory part number to identify both parts and assemblies. Therefore, the coding scheme used in Figure 8.1 cannot be used both to identify inventory and to show assembly hierarchy. This assembly hierarchy has been redrawn in Figure 8.2 using inventory part numbers. At least two indexes would be required in this example. In one case we must be able to start with the highest assembly and find all the subassemblies and parts required to build that assembly. This is illustrated by solid lines in Figure 8.3, which is a typical bill of material explosion. In a second problem we start with a part number and seek all the assemblies where the part is used, which might be necessary when a part number is changed and all appropriate records in the assembly file have to be updated simultaneously.

DATA BASE

Most of the data elements in the management system will be used in several functions for various types of outputs. This has led many organizations, over a period of time, to construct several files which contain duplicate information. Data about employees are frequently cited as an example. There might be separate, self-sustaining files for payroll, personnel, benefits, qualifications, and so on. There would be much duplicate data in these files, especially in the area of basic identification like name, age, home address, and seniority. The disadvantage is twofold. First, it requires unnecessary storage capacity; more important, however, it is

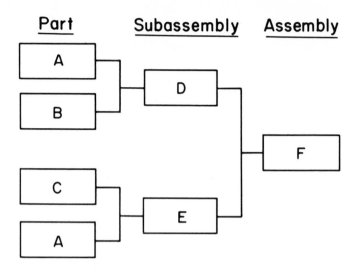

Figure 8.2. Assembly hierarchy by part number

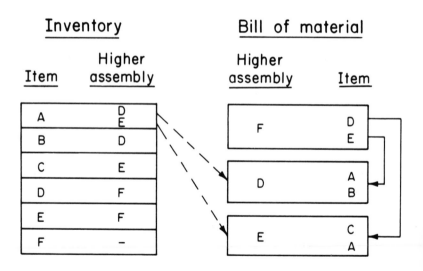

Figure 8.3. Bill of material index

difficult and expensive to maintain. Whenever any fact about an employee changes, all affected records must be changed. With independent files this means separate forms and procedures for each. Thus, it is almost impossible to keep several independent files synchronized.

The principle of single-source master files solves most of these problems. The single-source file consolidates all facts about every employee into one file. All functional programs such as payroll and personnel, which need employee data, would use this file. When a change occurs, the information in this file is updated only once (see Figure 8.4). In this way file maintenance cost is minimized, and all departments would have accurate and current data with minimum storage cost.

When the thinking behind the single-source file is carried a step further, the concept of the data base emerges. In this concept there is a consolidation of all files. The database concept, however, is more than just a collection of files. The term denotes a commonality of data and a standardization of the methodology employed in the maintenance and retrieval of data. In its broadest form the concept involves a system where all information received is immediately classified and cross-indexed and deposited in a massive storage facility. All functional programs would go to this facility and withdraw the data they require, as illustrated in Figure 8.5. Hence the names data base, data bank, or data-management system.

As with the single-source file, the data base is constructed along logical lines, not functional lines. There may be several major subjects of data constructed along the mainstream activities discussed in the Chapter 6. There might be subsets for such categories as employees, inventory, customers, and policy and plans. A major difference between the single-source file and the data base is the interaction between the major

127

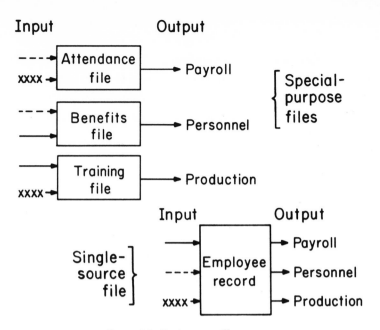

Figure 8.4. Single-source file concept

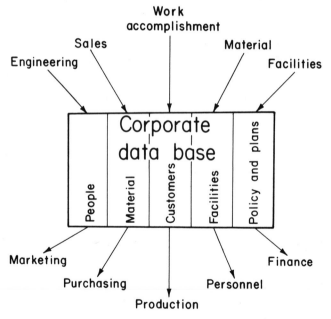

Figure 8.5. Data base concept

subsets in the data base. For example, if we wished to have a description of the equipment an employee was qualified to operate, we would not find it in the employee file; it would merely point to the location in the facilities file where we could find it.

When the data-base concept and its associated data-management system are considered, there are generally three components implied: (1) standardized creation and maintenance of records, (2) inquiry capabilities, and (3) report-generation.

The problems of file maintenance were discussed under data elements. The data-base concept involves the same considerations but perhaps at their most sophisticated level. Inquiry capabilities envision a user interrogating the computer data base from a remote terminal, which will be discussed in some detail in Chapter 9 on information retrieval.

The aspect of report generation deserves more comment here. With a data base most of the routine periodic reports are still generated by programs developed by programmers in a conventional manner. The only difference would be that application programs would not develop their own files. This would be the responsibility of the data base. The major innovation in the data-base concept is the use of a simplified programming language which could be handled by anyone needing a special report. It would work something like this: The person who needs the report prepares a few simple control statements which describe the report to the data-management system; the data-management system interprets the request, withdraws the appropriate information from the data base, and prepares the report. The advantage is obvious: management has rapid access to a variety of information without the intermediary assistance of a programmer. It is this advantage, however, that creates much of the complexity and sophistication required of the

129

data-management system. Data elements must be extensively indexed, and elaborate software is needed to interpret the requests and generate the required reports. Considerations such as these cause the data base to have a significantly greater computer overhead than more conventional methods. The greater cost is most often offset by the improved information content and availability.

STORAGE DEVICES

The management information system requires extensive hardware capabilities to store great amounts of data. There are many types of peripheral equipment available today to store data, each with its strengths and weaknesses. The proper selection of this equipment can have significant impact on the cost of acquiring and operating the system.

Some of the major categories of devices are shown in Figure 8.6. Many ingenious variations are marketed, and new developments are constantly introduced. Nevertheless, the limitations of memory capabilities continue to be the major equipment problem in developing large systems. It is not unrealistic to expect technological breakthroughts in this area to greatly enhance the potential and economic appeal of larger management information systems.

SUMMARY

The development of the basic design for storing data is a series of tradeoffs. The desire to minimize storage costs must be compared to the loss in flexibility. The desire to minimize processing costs must be compared to the desire to minimize data-collection and data-retrieval costs. The con-

Description	Capabilities	Use
Core Small ferrous "doughnuts" which may be magnetized by wires strung through each core	Data may be rapidly and directly written into and read from any core location; quite expensive in terms of cost per character	Primarily used as the main storage of the central processor for working storage of programs in process; infrequently used for auxiliary mass storage
Disks and drums Rotating surfaces which may be magnetized by stationary heads located next to the surface	Disks and drums allow direct access to data but are somewhat slower than core; also considerably less expensive in terms of cost per character	Used to store the bulk of the data frequently or randomly required by the system
Magnetic tape Reels of tape which may have data magnetically recorded on the surface (similar to sound recording tape)	Tape must be recorded and read sequentially and therefore has very slow access to data; relatively inexpensive means of storing large amounts of data	Used for information which is infrequently required, such as historical or backup records
Photographic process Photographic processes, including conventional microfilm, where images may be recorded directly from computer-stored data	Inexpensive way of storing quantities of information, although data cannot be processed or updated once recorded; in some systems the computer may retrieve and display specific records	Used for archival, historical, and catalog-type data; also graphs, drawings, etc.

Figure 8.6. Storage devices

131

cept of the data bank seems to provide the best solution to the problem, for all information is reported only once and is stored at a basic level. All functional applications then look to this data base as the source of all the data which will be processed in the individual application programs. This satisfies several design requirements for information storage—minimal cost of collecting and storing information; timely, accurate, and consistent data; and flexibility for systems expansion and changing organizational needs.

9

Information Retrieval

THE COMMUNICATION between man and computer is perhaps the most difficult aspect of any large information system. Unfortunately, this aspect is often one of the most neglected areas in the design of management systems. Vast amounts of time and talent are assigned to the evaluation of hardware, the derivation of mathematical models, and similar developments, but all too often the output design is almost an afterthought.

Perhaps one reason for this oversight has been the historical limitations of computers. Traditionally, they could calculate much faster than they could print the results. This no longer needs to be true. Modern computers with advanced operating systems and sophisticated peripheral equipment offer great versatility in output techniques. Central facilities not only include high-speed printers capable of producing great volumes of printed material, but they also provide a variety of other forms. Computers can produce punched cards, plot graphs, and prepare microfilm and other special types of output. The computer can now provide more data

133

than anyone can possibly use. The system designer must find ways of reducing this mass to useful proportions.

By far the most significant technical advance has been the development of remote input and output terminals, which allow messages to be printed in the work area. A manager can interrogate the computer from his office and have his answer returned immediately. Visual presentations are becoming common. Television-type screens (CRT) can provide both text and graphics. Although present screens are small, there is no reason not to expect large color displays suitable for group presentations in the not too distant future.

The designer's problem is now one of making the best selection from the means available. This selection of output methodology and the design of meaningful messages have become important to the success of the information system. There are, however, few pragmatic rules and little historical precedence for the designer. In this chapter we will provide a few guidelines to aid the designer in this task.

OBJECTIVES

With the growth of available data and the increasing power of modern computers, it is possible to completely flood people with data. Not only is this unnecessary, but too much data rapidly becomes incomprehensible and no one is much better off than he was before. The problem is to discriminate between all the data available and the data which the manager needs and can use. Some factors about information may provide insights into the solution of this problem.

Information theory, originally developed by communication engineers, makes a distinction between data and information. Information is that part of the data which can be used to increase knowledge—that which is unexpected.

Conversely, if a message is completely predictable, no information is gained by receiving it. The obective, of course, in designing management reports is to minimize the data which simply identify the situation and maximize the information or news content. (The old saying, "No one wants yesterday's newspaper," is appropriate here.)

The problem is compounded because the computer must communicate with a human manager, not another machine. While it is generally conceded that the human brain can process data with extraordinary agility, it is also recognized that man's input is limited. Most information is transmitted visually, generally through the printed document, where the data are subject to widely varying reading and comprehension rates. The management system must therefore be selective in the information that is transmitted and present the man only with that amount which he needs to do his job. People do display considerable ability in recognizing patterns and trends, and for this reason graphic presentations can be effective.

The problem is further compounded by the fact that an organization will not require the same information at all times. For example, a process that is out of control will require considerably more detailed data to bring it into control than will be required to maintain control once it is achieved. For another example, consider the information that would be required to evaluate a major policy change or facility expansion—information which would not normally be demanded. In these instances the information system may possess the required data but would not necessarily prepare reports periodically.

DOCUMENT DESIGN

The printed document continues to be the major means of communication between the computer and the manager. The ability of the manager or other user to efficiently utilize the various documents may well be a deciding factor in the overall performance of the total system. It is therefore important that careful consideration be given to the actual design of reports, in terms of both data content and format. There are many presentation methods and techniques available to the system designer, and they must be tailored to the individual requirements of the specific application. The possibilities seem to be limited only by the ingenuity of the designer.

Data Content

One of the first things to consider is the data content of the document. With any specific purpose and set of data, there are several methods of organizing the output. The design objective is, of course, to provide the required "information" with a minimum of superfluous data. The user should expend a minimum of effort identifying the situation and should be able to concentrate upon the message of the document—in effect, the information content. A few ways that information content may be improved are illustrated below.

Standards. Comparison of actual performance to a standard will provide a frame of reference which can make data more meaningful to the user, as illustrated in Figure 9.1. Standards available within an organization may be both formal and informal. Some, such as labor standards and production schedules, can be quite rigorous. Others, such

136

LABOR PERFORMANCE - MARCH
METAL WORKING SHOPS
000 OMITTED

REPORT NBR. 8962
MARCH 4, 1969
PAGE 1

YEAR TO DATE			DESCRIPTION	MONTH		
ACT.	VAR.	PERF.		ACT.	VAR.	
			PRODUCTIVE LABOR			
6025	195	97%	GRINDER SHOP	1985	58	97%
4654	136	97	PLATING SHOP	1551	51	97
4464	214	95	LATHE SHOP	1488	61	96
9457	408	96	WELD SHOP	3152	108	97
14461	812	94	MILL SHOP	4820	220	95
39061	1765	96%	PERFORMANCE	12996	490	96%
			INDIRECT LABOR			
402	67	83%	GRINDER SHOP	133	18	87%
625	68	89	PLATING SHOP	209	25	88
575	62	89	LATHE SHOP	192	20	90
862	151	82	WELD SHOP	288	47	84
1858	236	87	MILL SHOP	620	69	89
4322	584	87%	PERFORMANCE	1442	179	88%
52784		95%	TOTAL LABOR PEFORMANCE	17595		95%
852			OVERTIME HOURS	62		
2%			OVERTIME RATIO	1%		
11%			BURDEN RATIO	11%		

Figure 9.1. Comparison of actual performance to a standard

as production quotas, budgets, sales forecasts, and similar "goals," may be less formal. Any type of standards may be used, provided they are recognized and understood by the intended user.

Summary. Summarization is the classic method of reducing large masses of data to usable form. Frequently only the summary needs to be printed, as illustrated in Figure 9.3. This is especially useful when the actual summary can be compared to an established standard. Perhaps the detail need only be printed for exceptions or irregularities, as illustrated in Figure 9.2.

Statistics. Many industries have developed ratios, measures, and statistics that provide meaningful ways to reduce masses of data to a useful form, as illustrated in Figure 9.4. Various statistics have also been developed in more or less standardized form by the various management sciences. For example, cost accounting has overhead ratios, overtime rates, labor performance, etc.; quality control has fraction defective, AOQL (average outgoing-quality limit), etc. These statistics can become even more useful when compared to standards and used in conjunction with trend analysis.

Trends. Summary information generally becomes more meaningful when compared to similar data from past periods. These summaries may take many forms, such as comparing year-to-date with current period or comparing the current period with the same period last year. Trend analysis becomes even more important when it can be projected into the future using valid statistics, as illustrated in Figure 9.5.

Report Format

A second consideration in document design is the report format. This involves the actual layout, titles, headings, and similar problems. This sometimes seems so mundane that it is

TO B.D. SMITH-FOREMAN

DAILY LABOR CONTROL
GRINDER SHOP
SHIFT 2, JAN. 20, 1969

REPORT NBR. 4549
PAGE 1

LABOR VARIATIONS

EMPLOYEE NAME	NBR.	VAC.	ABSN.	IRREG.HRS.	REASON
O.A.DAVIS	31333		8.0		SICK
W.W.WATER	40719		8.0		EMERGENCY
D.E.ELLIS	51766		8.0		UNAUTHORIZED
J.E.JAMES	61116		8.0		SICK
P.D.PAULS	86576	8.0			
O.M.DARNELL	91002	8.0			
J.R.SMITH	40355	8.0			
J.J.JONES	18972			2.0	NO MESSAGE AT END OF SHIFT
L.D.DINGLE	65187			1.7	TASK LN.NBR.NOT ON FILE FOR SHAX001 C/N JRB7
G.H.SPRATT	89722			8.0	NO MESSAGE AT END OF SHIFT
TOTAL		24.0	32.0	11.7	

EMPLOYEE DETAIL
J.J. JONES 18972

ITEM	CTL.	POS.	LN.	M/HRS.	TIME	IRREGULARITY
RODX017	PAT8	GSO2	12	3.5	10.50	
SHAX001	JRB7	GSO2	03	.3	11.30	
SHAX147	LBT2	GSO2	08	2.2	13.50	
				2.0		NO MSG END OF SHIFT

Figure 9.2. Exception printing of detail

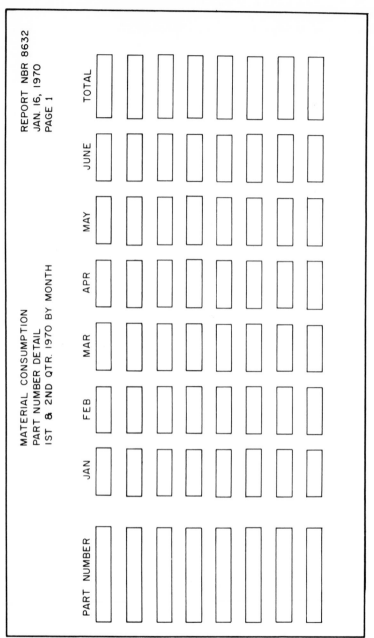

Figure 9.3. Tabular report format

QUALITY ASSURANCE
FRACTION DEFECTIVE CHART
PRODUCT GROUP B692

REPORT NBR. 9623
JAN. 19, 1969
PAGE 1

PERCENT DEFECTIVE																			
2.0																			
1.5								XXX	XXX										
1.0						XXX	XXX	XXX	XXX	XXX	XXX	XXX	XXX	XXX					
0.5		XXX	XXX	XXX	XXX	XXX	XXX	XXX	XXX	XXX	XXX	XXX	XXX	XXX	XXX	XXX			
	XXX	XXX	XXX	XXX	XXX	XXX	XXX	XXX	XXX	XXX	XXX	XXX	XXX	XXX	XXX	XXX			

DATE	8/18	9/01	9/15	9/29	10/13	10/27	11/10	11/24	12/08	12/22	1/05	1/19
PERCENT DEFECTIVE	0.69	0.94	0.81	1.03	1.17	1.51	1.39	1.23	0.97	1.11	0.82	0.69

Figure 9.4. Computer-prepared bar chart

141

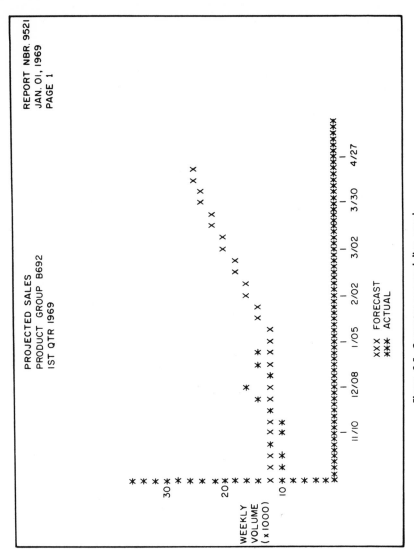

Figure 9.5. Computer-prepared line graph

overlooked. The objective is quite simple—to allow the manager to quickly recognize the document and efficiently interpret the information presented. The following guidelines may be used.

Standardization. There should be a degree of continuity between all the various reports presented to the manager by the system. There should be standardization of report titles and report numbers so that a person can immediately recognize a document's purpose and scope. Such essential identification as dates, times, and page numbers should be represented in a standard manner, and terms, codes, and abbreviations should be standardized. If this is not done, a person may, in effect, be forced to learn a new language for each report, or even more serious, he may be misled by similar terms with different meanings. This is not to imply that the presentation of the data should be standardized. Quite the contrary, the presentation method should fit the requirements of the information to be transmitted.

Data Presentation. The visual impact and readability of a document are largely matters of style and composition. The simple act of excluding unnecessary data helps. The use of graphs and charts can be effective in presenting data, especially historic and trend information. People are naturally adept at recognizing patterns in graphic data which would elude all but the most careful statistical analysis. A surprisingly large variety of graphic presentations can be made, even by a regular line printer. Some examples are shown in Figures 9.4 and 9.5. Of course, special plotters produce much more complex graphics. CRT's (cathode ray tubes) are also versatile in this area.

Information Cataloging. For information to be useful, it must be available to the people who need it when they need it. A report- or information-cataloging system of some type is necessary to be sure that all members of an organiza-

143

tion can determine what information is available and how to obtain it. The catalog of reports may also lessen the requests for duplicate data from several departments simply because they did not know it was available elsewhere. Where remote terminals are not used, a working document-distribution system is essential. System design may aid by printing the name and address of the intended user on both routine reports and special requests or inquiries.

Convenience. The convenience to the user is a rather intangible factor, but it can significantly enhance the acceptance of the system. Using names instead of codes is frequently a valuable aid to the user. People's names are especially important. Most important, however, are reports that may be used by managers as they are prepared by the computer. Computer reports that must be additionally processed not only waste effort but, more important, delay availability. Timely decisions depend on current data.

EXCEPTIONS

Another way of reducing the amount of data a manager must review is exception reporting. Here it is assumed that a process which performs normally is satisfactory and does not require managerial attention. It is those processes that are not performing normally or are "out of control" on which the manager must concentrate his attention. This, in theory at least, assumes that the organization knows what the normal behavior of all its processes is. As this is not always the case, exception reporting must be approached with a good deal of discretion and judgment. There are several techniques that are popularly classed as exception reporting.

Statistical Control

The decision techniques pioneered by statistical quality control can be applied to many other situations. This technique is based upon the principle that a process "in control" will have predictable patterns of deviation about the mean. Therefore, limits can be set for the expected behavior of the process. If a sample of data (month, week, day) exceeds these limits, it can be assumed that the process is not operating in the standard pattern and therefore represents an exception. Before application of this technique, it is essential that the process represent a statistically stable situation (in control). Otherwise, effort will be wasted investigating exceptions which really do not represent a change in the process.

Arbitrary Limit

Frequently, it is not possible or practical to use statistical techniques. However, limits based upon experience may be established in other ways. For example, a foreman may know that if his work load has exceeded the plan by some value, he can no longer recover by normal options (i.e., overtime) and must make alternate plans. In this case the value could be used as a limit. This is known as the heuristic approach. The key to the successful use of arbitrary limits is a rational reason for establishing the limit, one that really requires the attention of the manager.

Top 10

The "top 10" type of exception philosophy recognizes that in many situations the importance of items follows an S curve, where a few of the items create most of the cost. For example, in an typical inventory, 10 per cent of the part numbers may account for 90 per cent of the dollar investment. In this case the data are arrayed with only the highest items printed on the report. The danger in this approach is that while continuing to investigate the high-cost items, which after a while are fairly well under control, the manager will overlook several opportunities for effective action among those items not reported.

DOCUMENT STRUCTURE

When a series of reports is designed for a total management environment, careful attention must be given to the structural relationship of the reports. There is both a vertical and horizontal structure to be considered, as illustrated by the series of reports shown in Figure 9.6. This series of reports represents several functional responsibilities. However, recognizing that the purpose of much of that data is

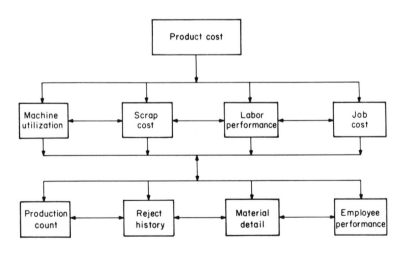

Figure 9.6. Structured report levels

for problem-solving, there is a definite interrelationship and requirement for compatibility. Reports of this type must be carefully structured so that the manager has sufficient information to interpret all conceivable problems and situations presented by the reports. The report structure should be such that investigation may proceed through succeeding levels of detail. For example, a problem discovered in reoperation cost may be caused by the job, the employee, or the machine. These lower levels of detail should be available for investigation, and the data at these levels should be relatable to the higher-level reoperation cost summary. The important considerations are

Identification—There should be a consistent method in the various reports identifying events and actions at similar levels of detail. For example, the same product identification should be used in machine utilization as in reoperation cost.

Hierarchy—Reports should be compatible upward and downward. If, for example, the labor-performance were by crew, it should be relatable to performance of individual employees who spent time on the crew and to the profit centers that were used in the product cost summary.

Sufficiency and Indexing—Sufficient information should be available to investigate the most likely causes of problems, either routinely or on demand. Through the identification, the hierarchy, and the report design, it should be possible to index from one report to another and track a problem to its source.

INTERACTIVE SYSTEMS

When the user may ask the computer a question from his office in normal English and immediately receive a reply in the same language, the information system is, in reality, online with the management of the organization. This type of operation is not as difficult to achieve as it might seem. There are several operating systems where clerical functions are handled directly with the computer. The airline reservation systems are an example, as are the systems used by insurance companies to maintain customer records. There are executives who have terminals in their offices so they may ask the computer for certain key status data. Time-sharing, whereby many analysts or engineers, each in his own work area, may simultaneously use a central computer to solve problems, is widely used.

These systems have various names—remote response, conversational mode, inquiry, retrieval, time-sharing, and so on—with very little common agreement on terminology. The methods, concepts, and needs they serve, however, certainly represent the future direction of interfacing the manager with the computer. They can, when properly designed, prevent many of the problems of shielding people from the information explosion.

There are several kinds of equipment, generally referred to as remote terminals or remote input-output devices, for transmitting information between the computer and the work area. Of the many types currently available, some are designed for specific applications, while others are general-purpose devices. New devices with unique features and capabilities are constantly being developed. All of them, however, seem to fall into one of three general classes:

Printers—Devices similar to electric typewriters can be used for input and output from the computer. While their speed is limited, they have the advantage of printed copy which can be retained for further reference.

Visual Displays—Devices similar to television screens can display either text or graphic information. They generally combine the screen with a keyboard for input. The visual devices supply information at a faster rate than remote printers and have more versatility in handling graphics.

Audio Response—There are several means to convert computer data to a voice response. This capability is generally combined with a telephone to provide an inexpensive though somewhat limited output mode.

Regardless of the means employed to communicate with the computer, the value is the usefulness of the data received. There are several degrees of sophistication associated with the responses can be provided. The simplest is the direct retrieval and display of a single record. This is the case when, for example, a clerk asks the computer to look at a customer record in order to answer a question from the customer or to add data to the record. Other similar uses include police officers checking a suspect's record, airline agents checking availability of seats, salesmen checking warehouse inventory, bankers checking currency exchange rates, production control men locating specific parts, brokers finding the latest quotations on a given stock, and salesclerks checking the credit of a customer.

The next level of complexity arises when a specific group of records is displayed. This involves a file search, which is a discrimination process—that is, a selection from all records of only those that meet the requirements of the class of records requested. A simple example might be a product-improvement investigation based upon customer service calls or warranty claims. One of the primary problems in a reliability investigation of this type is the sorting of information for discovery of patterns. If all the information from the warranty claims were in a computer file, the reliability engineer would be able to call for a report containing specific types of problems—for example, the failures of bearings on

149

Model K292 over the past three months, sorted by production sequence number. This type of retrieval demands well-structured files. Not only must the desired data be in the files, but they must also be organized and indexed so the computer may retrieve them in the desired form. This places a stringent requirement on the coding and classifying of data. Narrative data, such as might be involved in a library or literature search, require some method of abstracting so that the computer can match the request with the documents' contents. The computer-retrieval programs themselves also become increasingly complex as the flexibility of the retrieval system increases. The syntax of the retrieval request must be simple enough for the user to easily present his need, yet rigorous enough for the computer to accurately recognize what is requested.

Online problem solving is a little more complex. This is a typical use of time-sharing and offers great service to engineers, mathematicians, and analysts. In this mode of operation the central computer has a library of standard mathematical, statistical, and technical programs. When an individual has a problem to solve, he may "call" one of these standard programs from his terminal, give the computer his data, and immediately receive the solution.

The standard programs may not, in reality, be very standard. Almost any repetitive calculation may be programmed and placed in the program library. In practice, the programs run the gamut from simple interest calculations to bridge design. A bit of flexibility may be added to the system, providing access to any part of the organization's data base for input into the standard program, thereby relieving the individual user of the problem of preparing source data.

None of the retrieval methods discussed here has been directly involved with the decision-making process. They have provided information and quantitative answers to some questions, but they have not directly contributed to the decision. With some types of information systems, it is readily apparent that the computer is online with man in the decision process—air traffic control or the air defense systems, for example. In other systems it is not so apparent, but the computer is actually making decisions that once were the responsibility of people. Inventory control is an area where the computer is used to continuously calculate levels and then "decide" when and what quantity to reorder, perhaps without human review. From these examples it can be seen that computers can be used to support the decision process. Whenever technology in an area reaches the point where the process can be completely automated, the design problems are minimized or at least reduced to purely technical ones. However, when the system must involve both the man and the computer in the decision, the design problem is not so clear.

The objectives of the man-machine combination might be quite simply stated—assign to the computer the repetitive decision tasks that follow definable rules and to the people the tasks involving creativity, imagination, or complex logic. In practical terms this, of course, leaves some real questions about what the computer can do to aid man in the decision process. There seem to be at least three areas in which the computer can be of assistance:

Alternatives—In many cases there are a limited number of practical alternatives. It is conceivable that programs could be developed to recognize these alternatives and display them to the manager or, conversely, to recognize what alternatives are not available. In a sense, this is what critical path network calculations do when they identify the activities that are on the critical path and therefore cannot be disturbed without jeopardizing the overall project. Further, the computer can be programmed to evaluate specific objectives (as-

151

suming it has access to sufficient data) and inform the manager of the consequence of an alternative under consideration.

Complex Decisions—In many cases a situation requiring a decision may be detected and displayed to a human decision maker. The situation may be so complex that the computer has no idea what might be the proper decision, but it may be able, once the decision is made, to determine whether it is feasible. This is typified in many machines and test equipment by a warning light that comes on when the operator attempts an impossible combination.

Tracking Decisions—In complex environments the computer information system may be displaying interrelated situations to many people and receiving decisions and status reports from many people. The system may record and monitor all these data and compare the aggregate to certain predetermined threshold levels. If one of the critical levels is exceeded, the computer may produce output that indicates this condition to a decision maker. An example might be a job shop production control problem—delays occur, items are rescheduled, priorities are received, machines become inoperative. When the total load for one class of equipment exceeds any reasonable production expectation, a notice could be prepared for an appropriate master scheduler.

SUMMARY

The problem of communicating information from the computer, a rather rigid and inflexible machine, to the organizational manager, a human being with varied and frequently unstructured needs, is obviously complex. There have been no rules, procedures, or formulas presented for solving this problem, but some general guidelines have been suggested. Perhaps the best way to summarize them is to pose a set of questions to be asked when developing output requirements.

1. *Requirement*—Is the information actually needed to manage the organization? Is the information directed to the right person or department? Is it directed to the one who must make decisions? Could the information be further refined, analyzed, or combined with other reports before preparation?

2. *Availability*—Is the information available in time to make the required decisions or take the required actions? How frequently does the report need to be prepared? Does the information need to be presented routinely, or could inquiry be used?

3. *Structure*—Do the reports in different time periods relate to one another? Can detailed reports be related to summary reports?

4. *Content*—Is all the information necessary, or is some redundant? Can any form of exception reporting be used? Is the proper use made of standards, trends, history, and statistics? Has graphic presentation been considered?

5. *Format*—Is the display as prepared by the computer ready for use by the operator or manager? Are standard titles, definitions, abbreviations, and codes used? Are names used instead of codes whenever practical?

In many, if not most, situations, the most efficient form of computer output occurs when the user has direct communication with, and some degree of influence over, the action of the computer. Information is provided only when it is requested and, presumably, needed. This can also be an expensive form of output if not carefully employed. These types of systems present some formidable design problems. The hardware itself is fairly impressive. Not only is an online computer required, with attendant reliability and maintenance problems, but it must also be supported by rather large random-access storage capabilities. In addition, there are the terminal devices themselves, with associated control equipment and communication lines. The system aspects—software, etc.—are just as impressive. The files must be structured in a manner that will allow logical indexing to retrieve the desired information. Information must be classified, coded, or abstracted in a standard and meaningful manner. The content of the files must be sufficient to meet the needs of the system, and this sufficiency increases rapidly with the sophistication of the system. The sciences underlying these information-management methods are in their infancy. Researchers are still struggling with theory in general and, more specifically, with actual applications. The concepts, however, are powerful, and are actually being applied in practical situations.

10

Graphic Design Tools
–A Survey

A WIDE RANGE of pictorial and graphic methods is frequently used in system work. Systems-oriented people will invariably draw some type of chart or diagram when either developing logic or describing programs or problems to others. These diagrams are essentially simplified models of the complex operations or systems they describe. Graphic presentations of this type are, of course, able to convey a great deal of information efficiently and concisely. But equally important, they also have achieved some degree of standardization which enhances their value for the many forms of documentation essential to the development and maintenance of large systems. Diagrams are also effective for the indoctrination and training of both management and operating personnel. Because of this overall importance, a brief survey of visual methods will be given here.

BLOCK DIAGRAM

When major elements of system logic are diagrammed on a broad scale, the diagram is frequently called a logic chart or block diagram. This type of diagram is a generalized form which may be used to model many different operations or systems. It is usually employed only at a very high level to show basic relationships between the major elements of a system. The block diagram represents the elements with rectangular boxes or blocks which are connected by lines or arrows indicating interaction or sequence (input-output), as shown in Figure 10.1. In addition to representing the relationship of major functional system elements, this type of diagram may be used to show equipment configurations and man-machine relationships.

FLOWCHART

Such information-processing procedures as computer programs generally involve a number of choices of alternate sequences which are hard to describe in narrative form. The flow chart is a pictorial presentation widely used to represent these operations. It is essentially a graph or map of any sequential logic process. The steps within the process are indicated by arrows showing sequence or direction of flow. The shape of the symbols indicates either the form of the data or the nature of the processing step. Brief descriptions may be written within the symbol. The symbols have been generally standardized, and some of the more frequently used symbols are shown in Figure 10.2.

The amount of detail that is shown on the chart will differ widely depending on the use to be made of the chart.

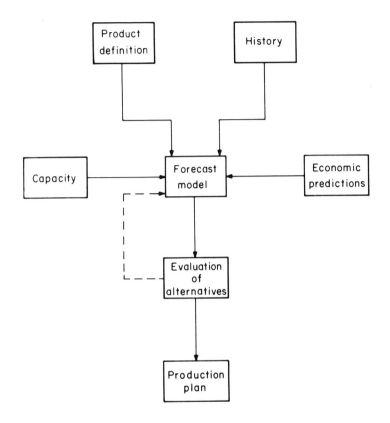

Figure 10.1. Block diagram

During initial design the system analyst may prepare a series of very broad charts to evaluate alternate methods. A programmer, however, may prepare very detailed charts before actually starting to write the computer program. Many other uses may be made of flow charts—for instance, general descriptions of the concept or scope of a specific procedure—and therefore, many different styles and forms may be seen. Figure 10.3 shows a procedurally oriented flow chart with a mixture of manual and machine operations. A summary level data-processing chart is illustrated in Figure 10.4. The

157

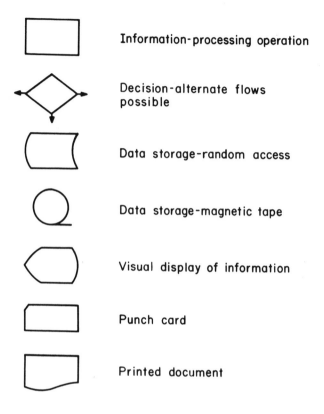

Figure 10.2. Flow chart symbols

flow charts used to document a computer program will be in considerable more detail; a very simple example is shown in Figure 10.5.

The flow chart has several strong points. The more or less standardized symbols provide a document which can be quite easily understood by all systems-oriented people, and the graphic form allows the presentation of a great deal of logic in a concise manner. The flow chart is therefore ideally suited to many levels of documentation and has become an

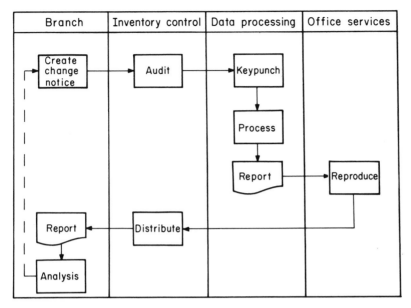

Figure 10.3. Procedural flow chart

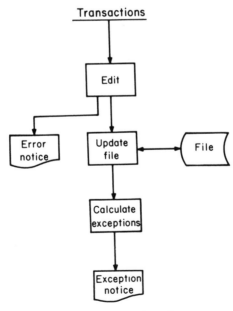

Figure 10.4. System flow chart

159

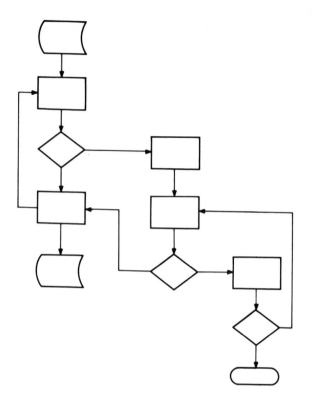

Figure 10.5. Program flow chart

accepted method of documenting completed programs and procedures.

DECISION TREE

The decision tree is another graphic method of describing a procedure or process where many alternate paths are available. Figure 10.6 shows an example, although many

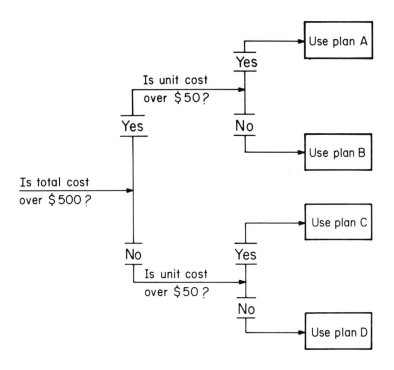

Figure 10.6. Decision tree

other forms may be used. The diagram need not be symmetrical; about the only rule is that from a single initial condition, the diagram should eventually lead to a terminal condition. The decision tree has many uses, such as analysis of complex logic processes or documenting various kinds of diagnostic procedures.

DATA MATRIX

A variety of matrix formats may be used to represent organizational and functional responsibilities in a manner that will provide an insight into functional system interacton and

161

information flow. An example of a responsibility matrix is shown in Figure 10.7. Through proper selection of activities and responsibility codes, this format can be tailored to the needs of many situations. It can be a convenient form of note taking in any fact-finding effort. It can also be used to analyze information flow, methods and procedures, or organizational structures for inconsistencies, omissions, or duplication in either existing or proposed systems. Another example of a data matrix is the input-output type of chart shown in Figure 10.8. This chart shows the flow of data without the constraints of time or sequence. It can be used to show such things as subsystem interfaces and data-storage requirements.

PRECEDENCE CHARTS

A complete class of analytical methods has evolved based upon sequential relationship of activities or events. Perhaps the best-known of these methods is program evaluation and review technique (PERT) which is widely used by the Defense Department in the development of weapons systems. Comparable methods are called critical path method (CPM), arrow diagramming, and networks. The principle underlying all these techniques is essentially the same: in most projects certain jobs may not start until other jobs are completed, but there are some jobs that can proceed independently. The precedence chart shows the order in which jobs must be accomplished. From this relationship it is possible to determine the minimum length of time required by the project and the jobs which are critical to maintain the schedule of the project.

A simple system design project will be used as an illustration. The project involves the following tasks:

162

Responsibility codes 1- Originate input 2- Approval authority 3- May be consulted 4- Use output	Department				
	Engineering	Inventory control	Process engineering	Production control	Production
Activity					
Bill of work			3	1–4	3
Bill of material	2	1	3		4
Tooling requirements			1	2	4
Job instructions	1		3		3–4

Figure 10.7. Responsibility matrix

Input \ Output	Inventory program	Financial program	Shipping papers	Back order program
Shop		●	●	●
Part number	●		●	●
Quantity	●		●	●
Date	●			●
Action	●	●	●	●

Figure 10.8. Input-output chart

163

1. Prepare preliminary designs or specifications

2. Prepare detailed functional specifications

3. Select hardware

4. Prepare computer programs

5. Develop operating procedures

6. Train operating personnel

7. Procure and install hardware

8. Test system

9. Implement program

Some of these tasks may be accomplished concurrently. Others must wait for preceding events to be completed. A typical PERT/CPM network, as shown in Figure 10.9, is designed to show these relationships. The point to remember is that only the sequence of occurrence is shown. Neither the length of the lines nor the position of the lines has any relationship to time.

The precedence chart shows much the same information. Figure 10.10 illustrates the same design project in the form of a precedence chart. The precedence chart is generally a more dramatic visual presentation and is not as structured in form as the PERT/CPM network. One advantage of the precedence chart is the possibility of showing partial concurrency and intermittent interfaces, as shown in the example between functional specifications and computer programs. On the other hand, PERT/CPM networks require rigid definition of beginning and end points.

However, time and resource requirements may be added to a PERT/CPM network, which may then be used for computer analysis to determine project length, resource requirements, and task schedules. This can be beneficial, especially in large projects with many interrelated tasks.

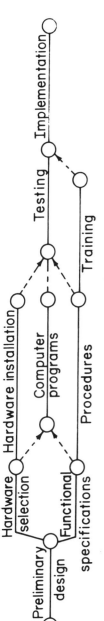

Figure 10.9. CPM/PERT network of a typical design project

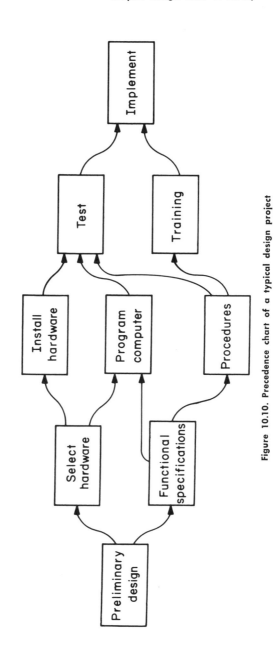

Figure 10.10. Precedence chart of a typical design project

165

DECISION TABLE

Administrative procedures often become quite complex, perhaps with arbitrary rules and exceptions, even for routine tasks. With these kinds of procedures it is difficult to prepare narrative instructions and even more difficult to be sure that all possible situations are covered. The decision table is a simple tool which aids in developing and documenting these procedures for both manual and computer programs. It is also useful when processes are essentially nonsequential, that is, where several actions can occur simultaneously. For this reason it can be very useful for documenting real-time computer processes.

The decision table consists of four parts, as shown in Figure 10.11—a condition section, a condition entry, an

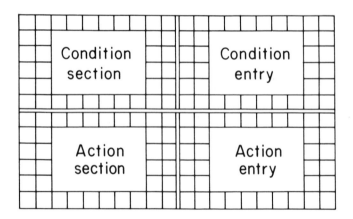

Figure 10.11. Decision table format

action section, and an action entry. The condition section lists all conditions or tests that must be considered before a decision can be reached: "Is quantity zero?" "Was the

166

shipment prepaid?" "Is the operation complete?" are examples. The second part, the condition entry, contains a "yes" or "no" result for each condition for all possible combinations of results (total cases to be considered). The action section lists all available actions that can be taken as a result of the conditions tested. An X in the action entry, indicating which actions are to be taken when a specific set of conditions is found, completes the decision table.

As a simple example, assume there are two lights, a red light and a blue light, which can be either on or off. In this example there would be the following possible combinations of results (cases):

CONDITION	CASE 1	CASE 2	CASE 3	CASE 4
Is red light on?	YES	YES	NO	NO
Is blue light on?	YES	NO	YES	NO

(It is not necessary to list "Is red light off?" as that is the same as a "NO" entry for "Is red light on?") Also assume that whenever the red light appeared, the required action was an emergency shutdown and that whenever the blue light appeared, the required action was switching to alternate power supply. With this information, a decision table such as that shown in Figure 10.12 can be constructed.

		1	2	3	4
Condition	Red light on	Y	Y	N	N
	Blue light on	Y	N	Y	N
Action	Emergency shutdown	X	X		
	Alternate power			X	
	Normal operation				X

Figure 10.12. Example decision table

167

This simple example probably does not demonstrate the power of the decision table. Many conditions may be tested, and for each condition several actions may be taken. The following set of hypothetical rules for a stockroom will illustrate a slightly more complex case:

When the on-hand quantity reaches a reorder level and if the unit cost is less than $50, the stockroom will automatically prepare a purchase order. However, if the total order exceeds $500, the purchase order must be routed to the purchasing agent for approval. If the unit cost is over $50 and the total cost is over $500, the purchasing agent requires a written notice so he can negotiate price. If the unit cost is over $50 but the total is less than $500, a routine purchase order can be prepared but must be routed to the purchasing agent for his approval. In all cases in which the reorder exceeds $500, the item is added to a weekly report for accounting.

A decision table for this set of rules is shown in Figure 10.13.

Decision table Reorder procedure	1	2	3	4
1. Total cost over $ 500	N	N	Y	Y
2. Unit cost over $ 50	N	N	N	Y
1. Prepare purchase order	X	X	X	
2. Route purchase order to purchasing		X	X	
3. Prepare memo to purchasing				X
4. Add item to accounting list			X	X

Figure 10.13. Reorder procedure decision table

168

SUMMARY

Charts, diagrams, and other pictorial methods provide a simple and effective way to represent ideas, logic, rules, and procedures. A degree of standardization of the methods associated with information systems has emerged through usage, and this has promoted the usefulness of visual displays for the documentation that is so essential to management information systems. These diagrams are used throughout the development, testing, training, and maintenance of the system. Because most of these techniques are so widely used and accepted, a general familiarity will be helpful to anyone associated with management information systems.

11

Analytical Design Tools
–A Survey

THE DEVELOPMENT of analytical management science techniques has been closely associated with the development of the computer. These techniques generally require extensive calculations which are economically practical on a large scale only when coupled with the calculating speed and efficiency of the modern computer. However, even with the computer these techniques were often limited by the cost and frequent absence of the basic input data. The growth of management information systems has made much of this information available, almost as a by-product, and has contributed to the increased use of more complex analytical decision tools. Similarly, the success of the analytical decision tools has created a need and justification for more comprehensive data, a need which has contributed to the growth of broader, integrated information systems.

These tools blend into the scope of the management information system in many places, as part of both the system development and the operating system itself. During system development these tools may be used to evaluate needs and alternatives, to design specific functional components, and to evaluate and test systems. They are also an essential ingredient in the ability of the management system to project and evaluate the impact of alternatives on the future operation of the organization. Without this capability the system becomes essentially a performance measurement and accounting system and does not aid in the decision-making aspect of the management task.

It is somewhat difficult to classify these analytic techniques, both because a specific technique may be employed in several places and because these techniques have been developed through a variety of disciplines. Ever since World War II such fields as operations research, applied statistics, industrial engineering, industrial psychology, management science, and similar disciplines have developed and used a variety of methodology which aid in the study of various functional activities when viewed from their behavior in the total environment—in effect, in their "system" environment. It is only recently, however, that these methods have been even loosely grouped together as a body of knowledge which can be used in the study of systems. The application of these techniques to the solution of system problems has become known as systems analysis, systems engineering, or, more broadly perhaps, the systems approach. This chapter will attempt to survey some of the better-known techniques and to provide a very general description of their usual applications to systems work.

QUANTITATIVE METHODS

The foundation of most management science methodology is the development of the ability to study the behavior of an operation or process without the necessity of experimenting with the actual operation or process. To accomplish this, it is necessary to build a model of the process which duplicates the key characteristics of the real process. This model could be physical (as in a pilot plant), but more generally it will be some form of abstraction. The abstract model will be represented in some symbolic form and manipulated using mathematical or statistical rules. Hence the term "mathematical model" is commonly used in conjunction with efforts of this nature.

Some of the earliest uses of mathematical models to solve business problems were in the areas of inventory control, quality control, and production control. Perhaps the best-known and most descriptive of these early approaches is the inventory control problem of minimizing total warehousing cost. Equations were developed to minimize such factors as the cost of ordering parts, the cost of holding inventory, and other costs. Later, probabilistic aspects such as fluctuations of demand and lead time and the cost of stockouts were entered into the solutions.

World War II stimulated the use of mathematical techniques in the solution of more complex logistics, production, and decision-making problems. Since that time the techniques have been refined and applied to an increasing number of operational problem areas. The body of knowledge which has evolved from this effort is generally known as operations research or management sciences. Some of the more common techniques are summarized in Figure 11.1. Of course, many different types of standard statistical and mathematical methods may be employed to build models for the analysis and solution of unique situations.

Technique	Description	Typical applications
Linear programming	A method of optimizing outputs where there are a number of inputs that are subject to control (if the equations are nonlinear, the solutions become complex but may be approached by other techniques)	Maximize profits of process-type operations such as an oil refinery, where the product mix (oil, gasoline, etc.) changes the profit potential and the raw material costs; also minimize transportation costs with multisource and multidistribution points.
Forecasting and prediction (smoothing)	Methods used to analyze historical time series data so that predictions may be made of values for future time periods.	Forecasting sales, inventory demands, operating costs, financial data, and similar planning information.
Sampling	The disciplined selection of a limited number of data elements from a universe is used to estimate character-istics of the universe.	Decision making in such areas as quality control, market research, auditing, etc.

Technique	Description	Typical applications
Quality control charts	Charts are prepared with upper and lower limits for a stable process; and where all plots are within the limits, the process is considered under control.	To control quality and detect assignable variation in all types of production and administrative processes.
Simulation	A model of dynamic process is constructed, frequently in the form of a computer program, to predict the characteristics of the process without actually constructing or operating the system.	May be used to evaluate a wide variety of processes or systems—for example, the job-shop scheduling problem where arrivals, delays, priorities, and operational times are subject to many variables.
Inventory theory	A series of models used to determine warehousing policy for such things as lot sizes, reorder times, and similar policies.	Used in any type of inventory situation to optimize total cost with respect to such things as carrying cost, shortage cost, and replenishment cost.

Figure 11.1 Quantitative methods

SYSTEMS ANALYSIS

As machines, processes, and organizations become more complex, it is no longer sufficient to design components that work when viewed individually. It is really necessary to design and assemble components in such a way that the total system accomplishes its purpose in an efficient manner. Therefore, the specifications for each component must take into consideration its relationship to all other components in the system. When viewed from this scale, it is apparent that most (if not all) real-life systems involve people in one or more ways. The objective of systems analysis (or systems engineering) is to evaluate the interaction between the various components of the system, including the human component, to determine the performance requirements of the various components which will achieve the overall system objectives in an optimum manner. Systems analysis is essentially a two-step process. The first step is to determine which performance parameters relate to the objective of the system and to determine the relative value of each parameter. In other words, what values should be optimized? The second step is the optimization itself, which involves tradeoffs of performance and function among the various components of the system.

The emphasis is on optimization of the total system. Many mathematical and statistical models will analyze one component (function) of the system. However, the optimum performance specifications for each component may not result in the optimum performance for the total system. This is especially true when the human component is part of the system. For a simple example consider a computer output. A printed output may be less expensive than visual display, but the visual display may reduce human error and search time to the extent that it is the least expensive system solution.

The systems analysist or system engineer may use any of the mathematical or statistical techniques previously discussed in his evaluation of system performance. He may also call upon specialists in these areas and other disciplines to provide information and evaluation of alternatives. There are, however, a few techniques which have been closely associated with the development of systems analysis and systems engineering. Some of the major areas are discussed in the following sections.

HUMAN FACTORS

The study of human factors deals with the interaction of a man and a machine in man-machine systems and how machines can be designed to accommodate human characteristics. In effect, it includes all factors—both physical and behavioral—that influence human performance in operating and maintaining the system. The physical factors may include such things as noise, lighting, and layout of the work place; the behavioral factors may involve such things as perception, discrimination, and decision making. Human factors, or human engineering, as it may be called, is a young technology with historic precedences in both experimental psychology and industrial engineering. It has, however, assembled a variety of additional tools from medicine, psychology, engineering, and other fields. It focuses upon a critical area in the development and use of complex systems, as the majority of the problems with these systems are attributed to human failures, errors, and the like.

The major efforts in human engineering can be grouped into three areas: (1) allocation of effort between man and machine, (2) evaluation and specifications for the interface with the man, and (3) measurement and evaluation of performance. The nature of the system will dictate the degree and sophistication that each area will have, but each will be represented even in quite simple systems.

Despite automation, there continue to be many things that people do better than machines and certainly many things that people can do more economically than machines. Early in the system development the designer must decide which functions will be assigned to the man and which to the machine. Design specifications may be prepared for the machines which are compatible with human characteristics. It is obviously more difficult to modify human characteristics than machines, although this may be the intent of much training and conditioning. Many of the problems with people in systems is the difficulty in specifying human performance and measuring actual performance against the specifications. This, of course, must be done before total systems performance can be estimated or evaluated.

RELIABILITY AND MAINTAINABILITY

As a system becomes more essential to the organization it serves, it is no longer sufficient for the system to perform properly when operating normally. The system must operate satisfactorily over a range of conditions with a high probability that it will perform its intended function whenever needed. As a system becomes more complex, the problems of reliability and maintainability become more critical.

Reliability analysis is concerned with the design of components and systems that possess inherent service life characteristics compatible with their function and use. It therefore involves the prediction of failure patterns and rates of various system elements and the impact of the combination of individual element failure probabilities on the total system. The economic attainment of reliability goals may lead to the evaluation of such diverse design philosophies as redundant components, derated design, graceful degradation of operation, fail safe/fail soft, and many others.

Maintainability is concerned with the time and effort required to detect, diagnose, and correct a failure once it has occurred. Systems designs that feature automatic testing and self-testing can significantly reduce downtime. Similarly, the human factors aspects of interfacing the maintenance man with the machine in terms of access, recognition of problems, and ease of repair are important. Maintenance must also be concerned with such diverse management functions as the design of tools and test equipment, the provision of spare parts, and the training of maintenance personnel.

The total performance of the system will be governed by a combination of reliability and maintainability. Economic tradeoffs are often necessary. For example, overall system performance might be achieved at less cost by reducing the reliability specification and improving the maintainability factor. Conversely, the cost of maintenance support, lost time, and so on may justify the expense of highly reliable equipment designs.

SIMULATION

Despite all the analysis and investigation techniques applied to the evaluation and design of systems, it is still generally impossible to determine how the system will behave in its real-life environment with any acceptable degree of assurance. There are just too many variables. There is need for broader methods to accomplish this task. Several methods loosely grouped under the term "simulation" attempt to fulfill this need. The general purpose of simulation is to reproduce the characteristics of a system in some environment other than the one in which it will normally operate.

Simulation may be employed during several phases of the systems design process. It may be used to determine the characteristics of the process that the system is to manage, to evaluate alternate methods or designs, or to test the system. Simulation may also be used as part of the operating system itself as a decision-making tool in routine management, where it is continuously supported by data available only through the management information system. It may answer the "what if" questions without actually implementing the proposition.

Various techniques are used to simulate an operation. Perhaps the best-known is the engineering practice of constructing a physical model. This model may be a prototype or pilot plant. On the basis of operating the model, a prediction about the behavior of the real system is made. Very similar is the simulation typified by dry runs, business games, and other training exercises, where the actual system may be employed and the environment simulated. This may suggest a close relationship between testing and training, and an economic benefit to be gained by combining the two.

There are more abstract forms of simulation using symbolic representation for both the system and the environment. Such mathematical techniques as information theory and queueing theory may be classified as simulation. However, the one method probably most closely associated with computers is Monte Carlo simulation, whose name is derived from the fact that many system parameters may display characteristics similar to games of chance; that is, the average outcome may be known, but the outcome of an individual operation (test) may differ greatly from the average. It is the interaction of these differences among the several processes (components) of the system that causes the uncertainty in predicting system performance. For every test, in the Monte Carlo method, a value for each process is selected at random according to the probability of that value's occurring in the actual system. The interaction of values for all the processes may then be evaluated for that individual operation (test). With a computer many thousands of trials may be evaluated very quickly, yielding not only the average system performance but also the extremes of performance and their probability of occurrence.

AUTOMATA

Computer-based management systems are becoming more complex, primarily because the systems are being used to automatically respond to an increasing number of the conditions the organization encounters. The more advanced systems assign more functions to the machine. As this occurs, the management analyst is faced with a series of new problems in the design of these systems. And he must seek more precise ways to quantify the management control and decision process.

The decision-making process is being studied by several disciplines, although each is incomplete and they overlap. Some understanding is provided by the engineering studies of feedback, stability, and control of physical systems. Mathematicians have added much to the formal solution of operating and optimization problems. Such fields as psychology are helping define the human components, their intellectual characteristics, and how they interact within the organization.

181

Computer specialists have advanced the understanding of logic and sequential processes. Much of this work has been broadly categorized under the following subjects.

Decision Theory—A series of techniques that attempt to describe how decisions are made and what information is needed for decision making.

Information Theory—The study of the information content of messages and the capacity of information channels.

Feedback and Control—The process whereby a mechanism (system) provides a satisfactory performance by using output to regulate input.

Artificial Intelligence—Studies focused on machines capable of behavior comparable to human mental activity, such as playing games like checkers, machines that display learning capabilities, and machines that solve logical theorems.

Cybernetics—A term applied to the common aspects of communications and control that appear in both living and non-living systems.

All of these subjects are contributing to the understanding of the management decision and control process. Each today provides principles, if not practices, which can be applied to the logic of management information systems. While many disciplines are contributing to development in these areas, unification of theory and practice can be expected and will provide management and systems analysts with new tools for the design of management systems.

SUMMARY

Quantitative methods are the backbone of the new wave of management philosophy and strategies. The use of these techniques is, to a large extent, dependent upon the availability of vast quantities of accurate and timely data which can be supplied only by an integrated management information system.

Many of these techniques also are used in the design of the management system. This system is a complex mixture of such things as computer technology, human factors, and management practice. The system designer must use each in its proper role and in the proper quantity. Precise methods must therefore be used to optimize the total system.

12

System Reliability and Security

THE ELECTRONIC COMPUTER, which is the heart of the information system, is subject to failures, like any other machine. The well-publicized advances in the miniaturization of solid-state circuits has effected lower cost and greater reliability among the present generation of computer processors. There is, however, much more to the computer as it supports a management system than just the central processor itself. There is a multitude of storage devices, output devices, and other peripheral equipment; there are such people as computer operators, maintenance engineers, and other support personnel; there are communication lines and terminal devices. All of these combine to produce a complex mechanism subject to a variety of problems all of which affect its ability to support the management information system.

Most, if not all, of these problems can be prevented or circumvented, although sometimes at considerable cost. Part of the system design task is determination of the level of support required by the system. These requirements must be communicated to the many specialists who are charged with the responsibility for hardware, software, communications, and all the technical areas. It is not the purpose of this chapter to discuss at length any of these areas; rather, it will briefly cover some of the kinds of problems that may arise in information systems. Because these problems are somewhat different from either conventional computer applications or manual systems, this discussion will, I hope, help the system manager to at least ask the right questions.

RELIABILITY GOALS

In most commercial environments it is economically impractical to utilize computer systems which are not subject to failure. However, as organizations become more dependent upon the system for operational decisions, the consequences of these failures become more serious. The system can fail in many ways; similarly, there are many ways of improving reliability. Because of the interaction of failure modes, there will be possibilities for engineering tradeoff studies at several levels to economically achieve the required system performance. Because these studies may well influence the fundamental design philosophy of the system, the required performance parameters should be considered from the very outset of the design study. The problem of reliability cannot be ignored, it must be dealt with.

The approach to reliability follows many courses. The first is the prevention of failures. This is accomplished by the proper selection of equipment, the availability of backup equipment, the use of rigid programming conventions, and the use of sound operating controls. When it is economically impractical to prevent failures, the designer must look to ways to contain the consequence of the failure once it occurs. The

186

first step in this process is rapid automatic detection of errors or failures. After the malfunction is detected, procedures and methods must be developed to minimize its penalty and duration.

COMPUTER CENTER

The central processing units are subject to random mechanical and electronic failure. There is also a need for scheduled maintenance and modification of the equipment. For both of these reasons, the central processing facility may not perform its design service to the system and therefore lessen the system's effectiveness. However, not all failures of processing equipment will affect the system adversely; for example, a failure might not occur at a critical point in the schedule, so there would be sufficient slack to make up the lost time. However, the more frequent the system response specification, the greater the probability that a processing failure will degrade system performance. When performance is critical, the design solution is usually the provision of surplus capacity and redundant equipment. Two smaller processors will generally provide better system reliability than one large processor. This is especially significant when the system may operate in a gracefully degraded mode—that is, with one processor operating to support only essential system capabilities.

The central facility is also subject to environmental failures. The computer is dependent upon electrical power, air conditioning, and similar utilities. Where the reliability of these services are unacceptable, the solution is generally backup equipment such as standby generators, an independent water supply, and so forth. The tricky thing is to consider all services—for example, power not only for the computer but

187

also for the air-conditioning, lights, etc. Other considerations may include water, natural gas, telephone, fire protection, and so on when they are essential to the operation.

The central processing facility may also fail to support the system through an operator error or a program "bug." This type of lost time is virtually inevitable but unfortunately is often neglected in system reliability calculations perhaps because it is difficult to estimate. Rigorous program testing and operator training may possibly reduce and control this.

COMMUNICATIONS

Online communications equipment is becoming increasingly more important to management systems for both data collection and information retrieval. They generally consist of several major components which often involve several manufacturers. This in itself may cause problems in the maintenance and servicing of the equipment. Figure 12.1 shows a

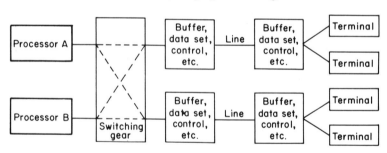

Figure 12.1. Generalized communications network

generalized communication network. On one end there are the comptuers which are receiving or supplying information. If the system is to be constantly online, as a data-collection system is, there must be two processors with the same capabilities. One unit will operate the system while the other is

188

available for maintenance, testing, and so on. Automatic switching between the processors in case of failure may be provided.

Next in the communications chain there will be one more "black box" type of unit variously called a converter, a controller, or a buffer, depending on the specific configuration. These devices feed data through communications lines (wires) to similar "black boxes" at the other end. The communications line may be privately owned, as might be the case with an interplant data-collection system, or be leased from a common carrier, as might be the case with communication between several cities. The input and output devices at the end of the line can be especially troublesome because they generally involve such mechanical elements as printers and card readers. Reliability in this area is achieved through adequate preventive maintenance and rapid repair service. If this is not sufficient, the general alternative is to provide duplicate equipment, although this can become expensive. However, a lot of ingenuity can be applied in the routing of trunk lines and the location of terminals. An example is shown in Figure 12.2. Where several devices are in the same general geographical area (shop, city, building),

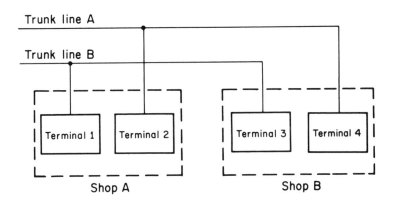

Figure 12.2. Location of remote terminals

189

part of the devices can be installed on one trunk and the remaining devices on the other trunk. In this way the failure on one trunk will not completely eliminate communications from that area.

Alternate methods should generally be provided for any communications network, at least to handle priority traffic. If nothing else, both input and output capabilities should be provided at the central processing location. For example, input could be handled by forms which would be keypunched and fed to the computer. Delivery to and from the facility could be provided by telephone, messenger, teletype, or facsimile equipment.

FAILURE DETECTION

In a complex system it is possible for a malfunction or failure to go undetected for some period of time. This can have serious consequences. Inaccurate information can cause the organization to make unwise decisions and alienate users and even customers and suppliers. Frequently, the longer the problem is undetected, the more difficult it is to correct. Specific internal system checks should be provided in the basic system design to detect any and all types of failures or errors. This should be an integrated effort which starts with input controls and carries through processing, communications, and outputs. An integrated design philosophy of self-checking and control should be established to ensure that the system does meet its reliability goals.

Self-checking starts with the input, discussed in Chapter 7. Further self-checking is accomplished by the processing hardware. Any time an exception condition is detected, a message may be sent to the computer operator through the console. Special diagnostic procedures may be run periodically to detect incipient failures or marginal component performance. The operating systems (software) of larger computers also provide a variety of controls and checks. These operating systems protect files and programs from unintentional alterations. They may isolate faulty components and provide alternate channels for transmission of information and may maintain logs of malfunctions or problems as an aid to maintenance personnel.

The computer programs themselves may have checks and controls built into them. The exact nature of the checks will depend on the skill and ingenuity of the programmer. There can be cross-checks of totals, where identical summaries are expected at more than one point in the program. Record counts are frequently used to be sure that all records are processed and that all records are passed from one program to the next. Various types of limit checks may be imposed where maximum values would not be exceeded in normal operation; for example, a payroll program might not allow a weekly paycheck in excess of $10,000, or a program might not be allowed to run more than 10 minutes.

The output of the system may be subjected to checking procedures. Most financial areas will be controlled by traditional auditing procedures. The computer has presented the auditor with some unusual problems where much of the audit trail is in language unintelligible to people. However, adequate procedures have been developed and can be employed. Other areas may have less formal audits. Simple manual checks, such as cross-footing totals of two reports, record counts, and samplings of results, can provide considerable protection against gross errors. Of course, an informal audit occurs every time someone uses an output. While this is a poor time to find problems, it can be helpful if channels exist to report the problem.

No failure should find the system unprepared. The steps

to be taken during the period of malfunction and the method of recovery and restart should be considered very early in the system design and should be published in the appropriate operating manuals. Relative priority of operations and responsibilities should be established for necessary recovery operations. Maintenance organizations should be established to routinely handle minor malfunctions of all types.

FILE PROTECTION

One of the more serious problems is the destruction of data in one of the major system files. In many cases it is impossible to recover this information, and at best it is frequently very expensive. There are many ways that file data can be destroyed. One of the storages devices may fail and destroy the data or may make it inaccessible until the device is repaired; a computer operator may make errors (write other data over the file, use the wrong input to a program, etc.); a program can erroneously instruct the computer to mismanage its own information or information belonging to another program. Because the variety of potential problems is larger, even though the probability of occurrence may be small, it is almost always advisable to provide backup or recovery capabilities. There are many approaches to the problem of file protection. Sound procedures within computer operations will greatly reduce the probability of file loss. Operating systems also provide various degrees of protection against inadvertent changes to file data. Beyond these more or less standard procedures, the protection techniques must be tailored to the type of file and to the cost of reconstructing the information contained in the file.

Status files, which are constantly updated, can have several degrees of protection. In very sensitive areas redundant files can be maintained on separate devices and updated simultaneously. Then, in the case of failure of one device, the second device could service the system with no downtime. A more usual approach would be to periodically "capture" (copy) the contents of working file on a second device and to save copies of all the input to the working status file since the capture. If there were a failure of the working file, the file could be reconstructed from the captured data plus any transactions that had occurred since the capture. In batch processing a procedure known as grandfather tapes may be used. The master file as it existed at the start of a processing run is stored on magnetic tape for several previous runs— hence, the terms "father tapes," and "grandfather tapes." When the run is complete, the oldest tape is released and the next oldest becomes the grandfather. From these tapes and a record of the input to them, a program could be rerun if there were a problem.

Static policy and procedural files present a special problem. In many cases information contained in these files are vital to the organization. A catastrophic failure to the system, such as a fire in computer room, could destroy all data in this area. These files could not be reconstructed except at great cost and probably considerable time. To protect against this type of problem, a copy of the file is periodically prepared either on magnetic tape or in printed form, and it is stored at a secure location, remote from the main processing facility. This does not have to be done frequently as the possibility of occurrence is remote, and some risk can be taken by not having absolutely current data. Some types of historic data and possibly the computer programs themselves may fall into this category and be given similar protection.

SECURITY

The general security problem with industrial information systems in no way approaches the military problem. In
fact, quite the opposite may be true. In many cases the
industrial system is designed to encourage the use of information instead of restricting or controlling its use. However,
the problem of security cannot be overlooked in any system.
The problem can be divided into two major areas—input
and output. Input considerations involve restricting to authorized people the reporting of data; output considerations
involve the controlling of access to confidential information.

Some control over the input is necessary to prevent
improper information from entering the system. This is in
addition to the normal logical edits of the system. In addition
to the random error problem, there are two more important
levels of improper information.

> *Nuisance*—Data may be placed into the system by employees
> to create errors in the system or to overburden the system.
> This can range from mischief to more or less deliberate
> sabotage. One of the best ways to eliminate this problem is
> to design the system so that this kind of action does no real
> harm. This eliminates the incentive (takes the "fun" out of
> the action).

> *Privilege*—Data may be placed into the system by employees
> to achieve personal benefit; for example, an employee might
> wish to falsify an overtime authorization or to alter an inven-
> tory balance to cover pilferage. Control in this area, of
> course, needs to be quite positive.

The control methods vary with the type of system. Many
data-collection devices include lockout features which employ
a special key to send certain messages; thus, overtime mes-

sages can be sent only with keys that are issued to foremen. Also, certain messages can be restricted to specific input device locations; thus, inventory write-off messages can come only from devices located in warehouse offices. The employee number is included in many messages from data-collection devices and may be included on forms or transcripts sent for keypunching. This employee number may be matched to a personnel file to determine whether the originator is authorized to take the action he reported. Another technique to ensure that the authorized person properly reported critical action is printing the message as the computer received it and returning a notice to the authorized originator for his validation. He may then detect errors or falsifications and take appropriate action.

When forms and transcripts are used for input, various batching methods may be used to control input. In this case a number of forms are assembled as a batch and accompanied by a batch ticket of some type. The batch control may consist of a count of forms, a total of some abstract number like the last two digits of a serial number, or other similar methods. Batch control as a security measure is valid only when some type of audit was performed when the batch was assembled.

For output procedures in an information system, it may generally be assumed that a person has a legitimate need for the information. One of the purposes of the system is to promote better decision making through the use of facts. Nevertheless, there may be some information that should be privileged. Therefore, in an inquiry or retrieval system there must be a way to limit the access to the information. Restriction of output can be achieved by controlling the input request. Certain types of requests may be restricted to certain output devices. Information may be restricted to a certain job classification, and through an employee number in the request, a check can be made to see whether the requester is authorized. Another problem is misuse of a retrieval system either through misunderstanding or mischief. This can be important when the retrieval processing is expensive. Control of the problem can generally be achieved by monitoring volumes of requests by location and investigating when abnormally high volume is detected. Charging the using department for the cost of the computer time required to process the request may also promote proper use of the system.

A completely separate problem is the question of fraud or industrial espionage. Every management information system contains much sensitive technical and financial data which would be of interest to competitors. It is always possible for a programmer or operator to extract this information, with only a limited chance of detection. When the computer operation and programming staff are managed in house, the usual management controls and industrial security should suffice for most organizations. However, where either programming or processing is provided by an outside contractor, this problem must be given serious consideration.

SUMMARY

There are many ways in which the computer complex can fail the information system. In general, each major failure mode involves a different and highly specialized technical area. There are some rather subtle technical tradeoffs between the various areas in terms of failure detection and prevention. The system designer's problem is the overall reliability of the system in terms of organizational needs. While each element within the system may achieve its own goals (or industry-accepted goals or manufacturers' goals, etc.), this does not ensure that the system will achieve management's goals. Overall system performance requires that such things as response time, security, emergency procedures, and similar reliability goals be specification considerations from the inception of the program. Although these areas may not all be problems in any specific system, they should not be taken for granted. In many information systems, except for very large systems, the problem may well be more one of providing a thorough understanding of the system goals within every area of specialization than one of rigid technical specifications.

13

System Implementation

THE SYSTEM DESIGNER must never lose sight of the fact that the system must be implemented, and implemented into an environment that may not be altogether friendly. The system must be tested in this environment; the environment in which it is to reside. People must be trained to operate and maintain it, and there must be an orderly transition from the old method to the new system. Provisions must be made for the continuous and successful operation of the new system.

The system design must frequently provide special capabilities to allow an orderly implementation of the system. The problems of implementation therefore should be recognized and defined early in the system design. Any special capabilities, programs, or equipment that are needed to implement the system must be considered as part of the total system design and total system costs.

SYSTEM TESTING

System testing is the final process whereby the system designers may ensure that the completed system meets design criteria and that these criteria meet overall management objectives. Then, as a comprehensive control of system performance, consideration of testing requirements must be a vital part of all design effort. Actual testing will occur at many points during the development cycle. There will be the need to test individual hardware devices, computer programs, mathematical models, operating procedures, and similar elements. Subsequently, these elements will be combined in various ways and tested as subsystems. Finally, it will be necessary to test the entire system in the most realistic manner possible.

The design of the test program will generally involve a series of economic tradeoff decisions. It will probably be impossible to conduct a full-scale test on an information system such as might be done with a physical system. Therefore, the test plan will include some form of simulation. The more comprehensive the simulation, the greater the probability of detecting an unknown deficiency; the cost, however, will also be greater. The increased test cost must be weighed against the consequence of a mulfunction once the system is in service.

In addition to detecting deficiencies and unknown problems, the test plan should detect these conditions as early as possible. The closer the implementation date, the greater the commitment to unrecoverable implementation costs and, therefore, the greater the consequence of discovering a major problem. The test plan must also contain a method for reporting problems as they are discovered and for initiating and controlling corrective action.

Testing will be accomplished at several levels. The lower levels involving small sections of the system can be conducted as soon as work is completed and therefore allow early detection of problems. The higher levels of testing must wait for several sections to be completed but will provide more comprehensive protection against complex interaction and interface problems. All levels must be integrated into a comprehensive test program. Some typical levels are:

Component Level—Each element of the system will be separately tested. Hardware components will be functionally tested against specifications. Individual programs will be run on the computer as each is completed. Forms and procedures will be individually reviewed for simplicity and practicality. Output documents will be checked for clarity and format.

Subsystem Level—At some point several programs, devices, and human tasks will be put together to check for compatibility and performance. This test point introduces the possibility of misunderstandings and misinterpretations of interface requirements. There may also be the necessity of testing a variety of possible output results which depend on variations in the complexity and timing of input.

System-testing Level—The total system is tested in as near a real-life environment as practical. All types of normal and abnormal conditions should be tested. For example, input data should be prepared by people with training and experience similar to those of the actual operators so that all expected input errors would be tested. The system response should be prepared by people with training and experience to those of the actual operators so that all expected input errors would be tested. The system response should also be tested under expected throughput volume.

Multisystem Level—As the so-called "total system" is probably never an instant reality, it is necessary to test each new phase of the system with existing operating systems. This will

201

check interfaces and compatibility in some meaningful manner to ensure that the implementation of the new system phase does not destroy existing functions.

TESTING METHODS

There are many testing methods which can be used, most of which may apply to several different levels of the test program. This can probably be generalized into two categories—simulation and operational testing.

Simulation Testing

Simulation testing covers a variety of techniques. Desk checking, which is primarily the intellectual exercise of mentally running hypothetical situations through a proposed system which exists only on paper. This can be done at many levels—for example, in checking preliminary design, in checking computer flow charts, and in checking forms design.

Laboratory simulation, where test inputs are developed and the output is compared to performance specifications, is another technique. One form of this type of testing is the use of test input to check an individual computer program. Another form is the generating of mechanical or electrical inputs to a hardware component and comparing actual response against the specification.

Mathematical simulation involves the automatic generation of data (perhaps randomly) which can be an input to a computer program or a decision rule to develop a response profile for that element of the system. It is very similar to the laboratory simulation except that a large volume of data may be generated economically.

Operational simulation is, in effect, a form of role-playing. A group of individuals assume the roles of actual operators of the system and attempts to manage the system from basic input through the use of outputs. The people involved may be designers or trainees for operating assignments. This can be an effective way to test major portions of a system if the test includes all the subtle problems of man-machine interaction, such as the use of actual procedures, forms, and devices in a real-life manner. This is the first simulation method that attempts to check the system against the system objectives; all the others compare performance to design specifications.

Operational Testing

Operational testing can also take many forms. The objective is to use actual operational data in an operational environment. The performance comparison is usually against an existing system or against actual management problems. Some of the techniques are discussed below.

One is the parallel arrangement, where an existing system is continued after the new system is implemented. If the outputs of the new system can be meaningfully compared to the outputs of the old system, paralleling can be a form of testing. However, frequently the new system represents such an advance in management technology that the outputs of the new and old systems cannot be compared. The purpose of continuing the old system is then a form of backup, and the use of the new system is more in the form of a full-scale operational test.

Another type of operational testing, a shadow operation, can sometimes be used where several generally independent areas, such as shops, warehouses, outlets, and branches, use identical systems. One of these independent units can be selected as test area. The new system can be installed in the test unit and results compared to existing system, much as was done in the parallel operation. The new system output may be used only for designer analysis with no disruption to the existing management of the test unit.

A prototype operation is similar to the shadow test in that one unit is selected for test. However, in this case the existing system is terminated when the new system is installed. The performance comparison must be against actual operational problems. Obviously, in this technique the system must not be so vital to the operation of the prototype unit that a system failure would destroy the effectiveness of the unit.

THE TEST PLAN

Because there are many options in degree, level, and method of testing it is essential to develop a comprehensive plan for all aspects of system testing, and this plan should be part of the appropriate system specifications. The test plan should systematically establish what is to be tested and who is to accomplish the test. It should also provide the method for reporting the discrepancies found and for managing the required corrective action. The test program should continuously compare actual results with design estimates so that system performance predictions can be validated or updated.

The test plan should define the performance measures and specifications that will be used to evaluate performance. Specifications should include not only hardware but must also cover other factors essential to the system—timing of outputs, sequence of operation, and response to input. The planning should include such items as volume capabilities, acceptable error rates, system reliability, and emergency operations. One of the more difficult areas to define will be the interaction between man and machine. The testing of operator errors on input devices, the proper completion of forms, the proper interpretation of outputs, and the practicality of procedures are examples of people functions which should be considered in the test plan. The performance specifications must be understandable and testable in all these areas.

To develop an adequate test program, it may be necessary to provide system outputs that will not be necessary after the system is in operation. For example, to evaluate problems, it may be necessary to print detailed lists of input transactions or lists of detailed data used to prepare summary reports. To test complex programs, it may be necessary to periodically print a status of the program and key files during the processing of the program. These needs must be defined, estimated, and included in the specifications and cost estimates. In addition to test requirements, consideration must be given to the problems, time, and cost that are invariably associated with "debugging," troubleshooting, and correcting test problems. No completion schedules can be realistic without allowances for these contingencies.

The detailed development of the test program must be a vital part of system design. There is much more time spent in various aspects of testing than is generally recognized. It is therefore essential that testing requirements be recognized early in system design and that test specifications should be included in all design documentation. If this is not done, it may be difficult to control costs and completion schedules.

OPERATING PROCEDURES

Because of the many people who will be involved in a management information system, it is generally necessary to have a formal operating or procedure manual. The development of operating manuals presents a unique problem. The manual should contain all the information needed by a reasonably qualified person who is generally familiar with the system. It should not be a training document. It must pinpoint only those points where people must take action.

The operating manual may, however, include many topics in addition to specific procedures, depending upon the nature of the system. There may be background on the system theory, computer description, policy comments, and similar general information. An especially important section is the description of the information provided by the system, either routinely or on request. This catalog of information must be carefully structured and indexed. For example, if an operator needs a specific type of information, he should readily be able to determine the document that contains this information. Similarly, if a man has a specific output document, he should be able to quickly find the description of data content, unusual abbreviations, and similar descriptions which may be necessary to interpret the report. This type of catalog and general information should be separated from specific procedural material.

The procedures themselves may be thought of as rules that people will follow when discharging their responsibilities within the system. Therefore, the procedures are not decisions that must be or can be made; rather, they are specific rules resulting from preestablished objectives and, as such, may be considered decisions that have been made

206

during system design and recorded for use by people in operating the system. An operating procedure then has several characteristics:

Specific Objective—The objective or purpose of the procedure must be specific enough to allow operating people to match the procedure to the problem at hand. This also allows the procedure itself to be concise and definitive so that it will be effective in terms of the person who must read it.

External Initiation—The procedure is generally externally initiated. That is, a condition, activity, or need not controlled by the system has caused the person to initiate an action involving the system. If it is an internally initiated condition that requires action on the part of operating people, the system should instruct the operator as to the appropriate action, and therefore no manual is required.

Serial Process with Terminal Condition—A single procedure terminates when the objective is reached or when alternatives or branches occur. Each branch itself then becomes a separate procedure. Therefore, a procedure is sequential and contains a specific end point.

It is important that procedures be readily retrievable. The individual in a man-machine system will require a procedure only when he wishes to initiate action by the computer or when there is a system malfunction. In either case there must be a simple way to identify the point where the man needs a procedure and a simple way to retrieve the appropriate procedure once the need has been identified. This demands a careful classification and indexing of procedures that is in phase with the operational requirements of the system. The procedure should tell the man his options and his step-by-step responsibilities at this point in time. In this respect the procedure may differ greatly from the documentation that was used in developing the system, such as flowcharts and specifications. These were generally logical in nature; the procedures are specifically operational.

TRAINING

The success of the system ultimately depends on people —the people who report data, the people who operate the computers, and, most important, all the people who use the system to direct the activities of the organization. Providing these people with the necessary skills is a major task. There are actually about three phases to the training program of any major management system. The first phase will introduce the system to all the people that will be involved and should start as soon as the objectives and scope are known. The second phase can start as soon as firm targets are developed. It will be in sufficient depth to allow operating groups to take all necessary steps to coordinate the system implementation. The third phase will instruct the people in actual operation of the system.

The first phase of the training program will introduce the system to all the people who will be involved with the system design or operation. This may include everybody from the top management to production workers. A primary objective of this phase should be to explain both the purpose and scope of the system. A great deal of fear and, consequently, antagonism can develop when people are faced with an unknown like the rumor of a new management policy. This is true not only of production workers but perhaps even more so of middle management, where cooperation is essential to smooth development and implementation of any new system. The introduction to the new system should therefore start as soon as there is something to talk about. This should

208

include not only objectives, benefits, and costs of the system but also any problems, as they are discovered. An honest and straightforward presentation will greatly aid in promoting cooperation and support at all levels in the organization.

The second phase of the training has much the same objective as the first. It is, however, directed at more specific areas than the first. For example, there might be a special presentation for the production control department, a special presentation for operating managers, and so on. In addition to developing general appreciation and support, this phase will also prepare the departments to properly coordinate the implementation of the system. It is necessary that they understand their responsibilities under the new system and integrate these needs into their overall departmental plans.

The operating instructions phase of the training is designed to teach the people the precise procedures necessary to operate the system. It may include the completion of forms, use of manuals, use of data recorders, operation of computers, and many other activities. The training may use a variety of media and techniques.

It should be remembered, when selecting the training method, that training is not a one-time occurrence but a continuous process during the life of the system. New people will become involved through transfers, promotion, turnover, and the like, and they must be trained. At least part of the training material should be available off the shelf, so to speak, in order to provide continuous training. Films, slide presentations, and brochures are convenient for this purpose. Continuous training may also be needed to reinforce the original training. It is often difficult to predict exactly what will be the most difficult procedural aspects of the system for people to comprehend and use. As the system error control design will pinpoint procedural problem areas after the system is in operation, training material should be modularly packaged so that only the required subjects are repeated. Very serious consideration must be given to who will prepare the material and conduct the training. The system designers are frequently a poor choice even for a small system. First, at the time when initial training is required, the system designers will be busy with testing and proving the system. Also, they will not generally be available for continuous training because they will be occupied with other projects. Another factor to consider is the increasing sophistication of the average industrial worker. Workers appreciate —even more, expect—attractive and well-prepared training material. The cost of training in terms of lost man-hours will also indicate the need for effectively prepared training material. It is often best to utilize professional help in the preparation of training material either from within or outside the company. The selection of people to conduct the training offers a wide choice. While professional instructors may be employed, this may be expensive, and it may be difficult to quickly cover a large number of people. One acceptable solution can be to use an on-the-job training approach. Supervisors may be given intensive training and provided with suitable training material and then requested to train their staffs.

There is often a tendency to overtrain. The assumption is that the trainee knows nothing about the system and that it is necessary to train him to a high degree of competence in all aspects of the system. However, quite the opposite is true. The average employee has considerable knowledge from previous systems or from general industrial practice. It is unnecessary to teach him what he already knows. The content of the training program should generally cover only what its new about the new system. Similarly, it may be unnecessary to cover all aspects of the system. Procedures or capabilities which will be used infrequently may require only general knowledge if the details are contained in readily available procedures manuals. However, whatever the content of the training course, it should include a restatement of objectives of the system and its advantages to the organization. The motivation to accomplish the job properly may be a more important factor in compliance than exact procedural knowledge.

Management instruction presents many problems, most of which are beyond the scope of this book, but a few points can perhaps be made. First is the fact that management personnel at several levels invariably require training if they are to effectively use the system. The operating managers must understand the capabilities and weaknesses of the control models. They must understand how to use the system to achieve their departmental goals. The information provided by a new system will probably be in different form and in more depth than in the previous systems. At a minimum, the manager must understand any new terms, statistics, etc., that are used. If extensive retrieval is utilized, the manager must know what information is available and how to obtain it. The overall objective of any business system is to provide better management. An improved system may provide the opportunity for better management, but this will never be achieved unless the managers use the system fully and properly. This may require a general sharpening of management skills for many managers. Managers with marginal skills may require extensive refresher courses. One area of staff management that should not be neglected is the people that provide the basic policy, procedures, and standards that control the system. For the system to provide tighter controls and assistance in decision making, it must depend on this static information. Thus, any new system will make greater use of this type of information, probably at the cost of limiting the options, alternatives, and initiatives available to the operating managers. The people who provide this information will generally be such specialists as planners, engineers, accountants, and similar people. The abilities and technical competence of these staffs must to a degree offset the loss of prerogatives by the operating managers. The staff specialists must be trained in the technical areas of the system that are the most appropriate to their specialities. But even more, they frequently must have their technical skills upgraded to match the requirements of the new system. It is also important that they be as highly motivated as the operating managers.

CONVERSIONS

No organization operates completely without procedures and systems, even though the existing procedures may not be apparent. The procedures may be no more than informal working relationships, but they are, nevertheless, the way the organization accomplishes its objectives, and will to some extent be replaced by the new system. However, most organizations do have some formal systems, and the new information system essentially will be a second-generation system replacing the existing system. A systematic plan must be developed for the conversion from the old system to the new system.

One problem might be the creation of a new master procedure and standards file. While this may be developed from the ground up by research and development, it is more likely that much of the required information will be available in existing manual files. In this case, special computer programs probably could be developed which would efficiently convert the existing files to the new system requirements.

The material, forms, information, etc., that are in process at the time of conversion can be a special problem. For example, in a production shop there will be many partially completed products in work at the time of conversion. If the new system requires a new routing form, it may be necessary to replace all the old forms on the day of conversion. Similar problems arise in inventory, maintenance, and service areas. Probably most systems will experience some form of in-process conversion. There may be the need for special procedures or even computer programs to accomplish this conversion. Whatever the system, it is important that the method of conversion be determined early in the system design. This decision will allow the definition of such conversion needs as procedures, programs, and manpower. The conversion requirements should be designed, scheduled, and controlled in the same manner as any other element of the system-development project.

SUMMARY

Every management system should be subjected to a complete operational test before it is released to the user. There are several approaches to the complete system test, depending on the nature of the system. The objective in each case is the same—to test all capabilities and functions of the total system in as near a real-life environment as possible. This testing phase is a critical aspect of the system development cycle, for it is the last practical opportunity for the designer to ensure that the system does meet the original objectives.

Every organization has some form of operating procedures, and the new system will undoubtedly be significantly different from the old one. All the people who operate and use the new system must appreciate and understand their

213

roles in the new system. This may well require comprehensive training at several levels within the organization. Similarly, the old methods must be efficiently replaced by the new system. Adequate provisions must be made in the design and the scheduling of tasks to facilitate any required conversions.

The success of the management system will depend on the attention devoted to implementing the system as much as, if not more, than it will on the design and hardware aspect of the system. People can cause the most sophisticated system to be unsatisfactory in actual operation. Conversely, people can make even a mediocre system work satisfactorily if they really want to.

Selected Bibliography

MANAGEMENT SYSTEMS

Hodge, Barton, and Hodgson, Robert N. *Management and the Computer in Information and Control Systems.* New York: McGraw-Hill, 1969.

McCracken, Daniel D. *A Guide to COBOL Programming.* New York: Wiley, 1967.

Orlick, Joseph. *The Successful Computer System.* New York: McGraw-Hill, 1969.

Rosove, Perry E. *Developing Computer-based Information Systems.* New York: Wiley, 1967.

Sackman, Harold. *Computers, System Science and Evolving Society.* New York: Wiley, 1967.

COMPUTER SCIENCE

International Business Machines Corporation. *Introduction to IBM Data Processing Systems,* 1967.

215

Chapin, Ned. *An Introduction to Automatic Computers.* Princeton, N.J.: Van Nostrand, 1963.

Sanders, Donald H. *Computers in Business: An Introduction.* New York: McGraw-Hill, 1968.

Sisson, Roger L., and Canning, Richard G. *A Manager's Guide to Computer Processing.* New York: Wiley, 1967.

SYSTEMS SCIENCE

Flagle, Charles D.; Huggins, William H.; and Roy, Robert H. *Operations Research and Systems Engineering.* Baltimore: Johns Hopkins Press, 1960.

McDaniel, Herman. *An Introduction to Decision Logic Tables.* New York: Wiley, 1968.

Meister, David, and Rabideau, Gerald F. *Human Factors Evaluation in System Development.* New York: Wiley, 1965.

Hare, Van Court, Jr. *Systems Analysis: A Diagnostic Approach.* New York: Harcourt, Brace, 1967.

Wilson, Ira G., and Wilson, Marthann E. *Information, Computers, and System Design.* New York: Wiley, 1966.

Index

219